India Studies in Business and Economics

The Indian economy is considered to be one of the fastest growing economies of the world with India amongst the most important G-20 economies. Ever since the Indian economy made its presence felt on the global platform, the research community is now even more interested in studying and analyzing what India has to offer. This series aims to bring forth the latest studies and research about India from the areas of economics, business, and management science. The titles featured in this series will present rigorous empirical research, often accompanied by policy recommendations, evoke and evaluate various aspects of the economy and the business and management landscape in India, with a special focus on India's relationship with the world in terms of business and trade.

More information about this series at http://www.springer.com/series/11234

R. Srinivasan · C.P. Lohith

Strategic Marketing and Innovation for Indian MSMEs

Springer

R. Srinivasan
Department of Management Studies
Indian Institute of Science
Bengaluru, Karnataka
India

C.P. Lohith
Department of Mechanical Engineering
Siddaganga Institute of Technology
Tumakuru, Karnataka
India

ISSN 2198-0012 ISSN 2198-0020 (electronic)
India Studies in Business and Economics
ISBN 978-981-10-3589-0 ISBN 978-981-10-3590-6 (eBook)
DOI 10.1007/978-981-10-3590-6

Library of Congress Control Number: 2016963418

Printed on acid-free paper

This Springer imprint is published by Springer Nature
The registered company is Springer Nature Singapore Pte Ltd.
The registered company address is: 152 Beach Road, #21-01/04 Gateway East, Singapore 189721, Singapore

At the Lotus Feet of the Lord
of seven hills

Lord Shri Venkateshwara

Preface

Strategic Marketing (SM) aims at achieving excellence in organizations. It is the cornerstone of improving productivity, profitability, and market sustainability while giving a firm the most sought after competitive advantage. Market dynamics, price, and customer expectations are pressurizing organizations to be innovative in all their activities. While strategic marketing is imperative to gain competitive advantage, innovation is the catalyst for further growth. Innovation is doing things differently with a constant eye on quality and has become the order of the day. This is all the more relevant to Indian organizations who have adopted strategies to compete locally as well as globally. Consequently, it has become important to evaluate the appropriateness of SM for achieving innovation. This book attempts to investigate how SM is influencing the innovation performance of organizations.

It has been observed that SM is extremely useful for any manufacturing firm to attain the required growth and can be used as a means where Indian firms can derive differential advantage. This is also confirmed by findings from the literature. Customer satisfaction is aimed through these strategies; competition and cost pressures are forcing organizations to invest in innovation. Organizations can achieve competitive advantage by constantly working on improved product attributes.

This attains greater significance as the after effect of the economic reforms, especially w.r.t. liberalization, privatization, and globalization, start sinking deeper. Many organizations and industry associations are also thinking on the lines that innovation is the need of the hour and focus on SM by organizations is to shift towards 'achieving excellence through innovation'.

In this book, a structured study has been done on MSMEs to bring out the correlation between innovation and SM in Indian manufacturing organizations. Indian organizations which were more traditional in their approach towards strategies are feeling the intense market pressure to modify their policy w.r.t. quality. The result has been a change to 'Strategy with Innovation'. The book examines the relationship between SM and innovation performance.

Entry of MNCs has created stiff competition to Indian organizations w.r.t. quality, product depth, and price. This also acted as a wake-up call to Indian organizations to provide high-quality products. By late 1990s and early 2000, a large number of Indian organizations had implemented many of the standard practices for achieving quality in their products and services.

Market competition is now making Indian firms to adopt innovation in addition. This demanded innovation in product, process, technology, system, and in almost all areas of an organization. These necessitated taking strategies and innovation together to derive benefits. Not many such studies are available from the Indian context. This book represents a modest structured attempt to bridge this gap.

Innovation is the basis for creating and sustaining competitiveness in the existing complex business systems. When planning a business strategy, it is necessary to have a proper understanding of innovation and the management process. The crucial link between innovation and SM, therefore, is the long-term and short-term strategies, which integrates the action of today with the vision of tomorrow. Innovation can help organizations to achieve the perceived quality as expected by customer from the offered quality.

Attempt is made in this book to identify the variables of strategic marketing which in turn lead to innovation performance. It can be useful to students, researchers, professionals, and also policy makers.

This book has been possible due to the efforts of Sagarika Ghosh, Nupoor Singh, and the staff of Springer. But most of all, our thanks go to the students and readers who have inspired the content and style of this book. Our effort will be successful only if this book helps them understand the importance and need of strategic marketing and innovation in the manufacturing firms to gain the competitive advantage.

Constructive suggestions for improvement of the book are welcome.

Bengaluru, India Prof. R. Srinivasan
Tumakuru, India Dr. C.P. Lohith

Contents

About the Authors

R. Srinivasan is Emeritus Professor, Department of Management Studies, Indian Institute of Science, Bengaluru, India. After his postgraduate studies in Engineering, he obtained his doctoral degree (Fellow Program) from the Indian Institute of Management, Bengaluru. Subsequently, he engaged in postdoctoral training at the University of Leeds, UK. He has more than 35 years of experience in both academia and industry, having served at some of India's most reputed organizations, including Tata Consulting Engineers (TCE), New Delhi, Administrative Staff College of India (ASCI), Hyderabad, and National Institute of Training in Industrial Engineering (NITIE), Mumbai. His nearly 200 research papers have been published in leading international and national journals and he has authored seven books including "Strategic Business Decisions: A Quantitative Approach", published by Springer.

Dr. C.P. Lohith is Assistant Professor, Department of Mechanical Engineering, Siddaganga Institute of Technology, Tumakuru, India. After completing his Bachelor's degree in Mechanical Engineering, he engaged in postgraduate studies in Product Design and Engineering and completed his Ph.D. in the area of Strategic Marketing and Innovation in the Department of Management Studies, Indian Institute of Science (IISc), Bengaluru. He has more than 13 years of experience in academia. His doctoral research work focuses on the topic "Impact of Strategic Marketing and Innovation Performance of Indian MSMEs". He has presented many papers at International conferences and International journals, many of which have been published in journals of renowned associations such as Institute of Electrical and Electronics Engineers (IEEE), International Journal of Business and Systems Research (IJBSR-Inderscience) and EuroMed Journal of Business (Thomson Reuters).

Chapter 1
Introduction to MSMEs

Abstract Indian MSMEs (Micro Small Medium Enterprises) are shifting slightly from low technology base products to higher end, and in spite of this drift, it represents a vast technological diversity. Indian MSMEs happen to be the significant contributor for the nation's economy. It is highly contributing towards Indian GDP growth by creating high employment and also manufacturing and exporting products. MSMEs are identifying niche markets and there by reach to a wide market space. It is also able to minimize the gap between urban and rural developments. Hence government of India is also keen in bringing out several initiatives to boost up the MSME sector.

The key takeaways for the reader from this chapter are listed below

- SSI transformation into MSMEs
- Contributions of MSME to Indian Economy
- Background for this study
- Objectives of the study

Keywords MSME · SSI · Entrepreneurship · MSMED Act 2006 · Strategic marketing · Innovation

1.1 Evolution from SSIs to MSMEs

Indian industrial policy regulated by industrial policy resolution of 1948 identified the importance of state in the upliftment of industries and thereby encourage entrepreneurs to start enterprises. It also became a regulatory board to see that guidelines and other policies are implemented by time to time. In order to curb the entry of multinationals into our industrial territory, a strategic planning such as regulation on private business, investment, land and infrastructure and foreign exchange needs to be intiated. SSI policies are framed during second five year plan. Equity as the guiding principle for SSI growth was chosen as the mantra for success during second industrial policy in 1956. Its main agenda was to see that SSI's

R. Srinivasan and C.P. Lohith, *Strategic Marketing and Innovation for Indian MSMEs*, India Studies in Business and Economics,
DOI 10.1007/978-981-10-3590-6_1

should accommodate large number of peoples as employees and offer a decent life to the people residing in rural areas. In addition, they also planned to see that there will be an effective and optimum use of resources such as skill, capital and human power which might otherwise remain unused.

1997 Policy Statement

Industrial policy statement of 1977 was formulated to see that the small scale industries grow to a greater state and also create conducive environment for its safeguard.

The important recommendations made were as follows:

1. Small and cottage industries can manufacture any products as long as it is manufacturable one.
2. The earlier limit of producing products by SSI was raised from 180 to 504 and then to 836 in 1996.
3. Tiny sector were given more importance and its definition says 'any enterprise started with an investment of rupees one lakh covering both plant and machinery in rural area having a population less than fifty thousand.
4. Entrepreneurs under cottage and household industries will be given due importance through a special legislation.
5. The concept of DIC (District Industries Centre) was to be introduced to cater to the needs of small industries in small town and villages. The main idea was to shift the development plans from cities to rural area.
6. Product standardization, quality control and marketing services were adopted for promoting SSI products.

Policy Statement

Ancillaries were given more importance during the 1980s policy statement. As a result of this, rural and backward areas were identified for the future growth. The inflation impact was taken care during the 1985s policy statement, which resulted in enhancing the investment ceiling for SSI to rupees 35 lakhs and for ancillaries to rupees 45 lakhs.

1.2 Small Scale Industry (SSI) in India

Any enterprise having a maximum investment of rupees 6 million covering for plant and machineries was considered as SSI. There was no minimum investment as such but the maximum limit was reserved for firms which exports. The limit of rupees 6 million was raised to rupees 30 million as a result of industrial policy changes in 1997. All the governments started adopting Gandhian philosophy of considering small scale sector as the main contributor and growth engine for the country. The special care was taken during all 5 year plans, since they realized that it will be the seed bed for entrepreneurship. As a result of this, it has a major share of 40% in industrial production and 35% of the total exports goods was from this small sector. In addition, it became the next to that of employment after agriculture. Around 14 millions got employed as a result of the initiative taken to promote small scale units. Trading and services (apart from few industrial services) were not considered under SSI classification.

According to MSME (Micro Small Medium Enterprises) third census made in 2001–02, this small sector was a significant contributor in Indian economic growth and roughly there were around 4.5 million MSMEs throughout the country. As per Ministry of MSME annual report 2010, there were 6.16 million people employed under registered MSME sector. Its contribution was about 8% of the GDP of the country, 45% of manufacturing output and about 40% of exports were from MSME sector.

The annual report of 2008–09 by Ministry of MSMEs says that there are around 6000 products manufactured by MSMEs covering both traditional and high technology based products. The range of products included food, beverage, cotton, textiles, silk, synthetics, jute, wood, paper, printings etc.

Liberalization, Privatization and Globalization has created an enormous opportunity and market space for SSI's to grow. In order to acquire this new market, SSI's needs to be innovative. As a result, the need of innovation to have a sustained growth, MSMEs are putting extreme effort to cater to local and as well as global needs. The policies and guidelines framed by the government needs to enhance the firm's capability to have a higher growth in the developing country like India (Lall 2000).

Existing literature says that innovations are taken care mostly by the small enterprises to a greater extent, though it may not be the same across the globe and among the firms of different categories (Lall 1992; Rothwell 1991). Over the time, only higher end and technology based firms were taken into account as per the innovations are concerned (Brenner 1987), and as a result of this small firms adopting innovations are not taken into considerations (Hausman 2005). In spite of innovations happening in the small sector, there are very few studies available in the literature.

1.3 MSMEs

The Indian small scale industries definition is not the same since 1950; presently the definition of MSMEs is according to MSME (Micro Small Medium Enterprises) Act 2006. As per the Act, industries are defined in terms of investment only as compared to earlier way of considering employment or output, investment or a combination of these three variables.

The MSMEs in India have seen an enhancement from "protection" specific policies during pre 90s to "export oriented" policies post 90s. There had been a longstanding demand from small industry associations, entrepreneurs, and related stakeholders for a single comprehensive law. To fulfil these demands.

MSME Act 2006 was notified by government of Indian in Oct. 2006. The act defined the existence of medium enterprises in India and existence of micro

Table 1.1 Categories under manufacturing sector

Manufacturing sector	
Enterprises	Investment in plant and machinery
Micro	Less than Rs. 25 lakhs
Small	Over Rs. 25 lakhs but not exceeding Rs. 5 crores
Medium	Over Rs. 5 crores but less than Rs. 10 crores

source Micro, Small & Medium enterprises Development Act 2006

enterprises in the act for the first time. It provided the legal framework to organize the three tiers of enterprises namely micro, small and medium enterprises. The MSMED Act started the term "enterprise" in place of industry and classified the micro small and medium enterprises into two categories namely manufacturing enterprises and service enterprises.

1. Manufacturing Enterprises—these are the enterprises which manufacture or produce goods pertaining to any industry and are defined as per investment in plants and machinery.
2. Service Enterprises—these are the enterprises which provide or render services and are defined as per investment in equipment.

MSMEs act as growth engine for any country's economic development. They necessarily create huge employment and there by catalyzes entrepreneurial thoughts among the people. It also helps in creating a healthy and crucial competitiveness among the firms and thereby to gain competitive advantage. The limit for investment in plants and machinery for manufacturing enterprises and in equipment for service enterprises as notified vide S.O.1642 (E) dated 29-09-2006 is mentioned below (Tables 1.1 and 1.2).

There exists an absolute need to fill the gap by suggesting suitable strategic plans to make the ecosystem to support "Make in India" initiatives of the present government of India. The main reasons for promoting small scale industries are stated as follows:

1. Small enterprises increases the economic growth and it is considered to be the labour intensive.
2. Due to the uniform presence of the small sector throughout the country, wealth is distributed uniformly all over the country.
3. Economic growth can be enhanced if proper financial infrastructure tuned to the unorganized sector.

Table 1.2 Categories under service sector

Service sector	
Enterprises	Investment in plant and machinery
Micro	Less than Rs. 10 lakhs
Small	Over Rs. 10 Lakhs but not exceeding Rs. 2 crores
Medium	Over Rs. 2 crore but not exceeding Rs. 5 crores

source Micro, Small & Medium enterprises Development Act 2006

Within the sector, both micro and small firms act as the green field for nurturing them and boosts up them to get converted into medium and large firms. As a result of this both developing and developed country consider MSMEs as the focal area for development.

Indian ministry of MSMEs consider MSME sector as the significant contributor and acts as an incubator where in the entire ecosystem is nurtured. At present, MSMEs is contributing about 9% of GDP's growth, 45% of manufactured production and 40% of exports. MSMEs are now also next to the agricultural sector when employment is concerned. Apart from this, about 50% of MSMEs are run by under privilege persons covering various categories including women, underlining the overall development.

The spectrum of MSMEs is widely covering all the different sectors starting from sub-contractors and the slow growing informal and unorganized sector to high-tech and organized sectors covering all the different fields. The available facts and figures is covering only the registered MSMEs, thus many of the unknown facts has to come from around unregistered MSMEs which is about 94%. If both registered and unregistered organizations are taken together, the effect will be much more remarkable as far as the growth aspects are concerned.

1.4 Contribution of MSME to Indian Economy

Considering the huge impact by MSME's on the overall economic development of our nation, MSMEs cannot be isolated among the different among the different significantly contributors. It needs to be properly nurtured and promoted by several initiatives and policies by both central and state governments. Presently the MSMEs growth is at a rate of 12–13% annually and contributing highly for the development. But there exists a huge competition among the MSMEs both in local and global scenario. The answer for them will be the innovation based technologies which needs to be considered as weapon for the success.

MSMEs growth should be an integral part of the country's economic growth and proper strategies has to be formulated for the overall growth. All the respective governments of the country at different point of time have suitably realized the importance of MSMEs and they have had good number of program and initiatives to develop small scale sectors. In spite of these initiatives and strategies adopted, there exist higher competition among different players both locally and globally. So government and policy makers have a great role to nurture innovative enterprises coming under MSME sector to see the bright future ahead. The contribution through industrial production and its corresponding GDP by Indian MSMEs are showing both ups and down with respect to the figures as indicated in the Table 1.3 below. This data clearly indicates that there is an absolute need for both MSMEs and the respective governments to take initiatives to see that its contribution is in the growing trend and there by enhance GDP's growth.

Table 1.3 MSMEs contribution-industrial production and GDP

Year	Total industrial production	Gross domestic product (GDP)
1999–00	39.74	5.86
2000–01	39.71	6.04
2001–02	39.12	5.77
2002–03	38.89	5.91
2003–04	38.74	5.79
2004–05	38.62	5.84
2005–06	38.56	5.83
2006–07	44.12	7.44
2007–08	45.00	8.00

Source Annual report 2008–09, Ministry of Micro, Small and Medium Enterprises

The MSMEs in India varies in terms of the size of the enterprises, the products and services offered, location and technology used. They produce diverse range of products which is used by local and international markets. MSMEs mainly manufacture parts and components to be used by large scale industries. They manufacture over 6000 products ranging from traditional to high-tech items in addition to the distinguished varieties of services being offered. The leading industry of this sector with their respective share is shown in Fig. 1.1.

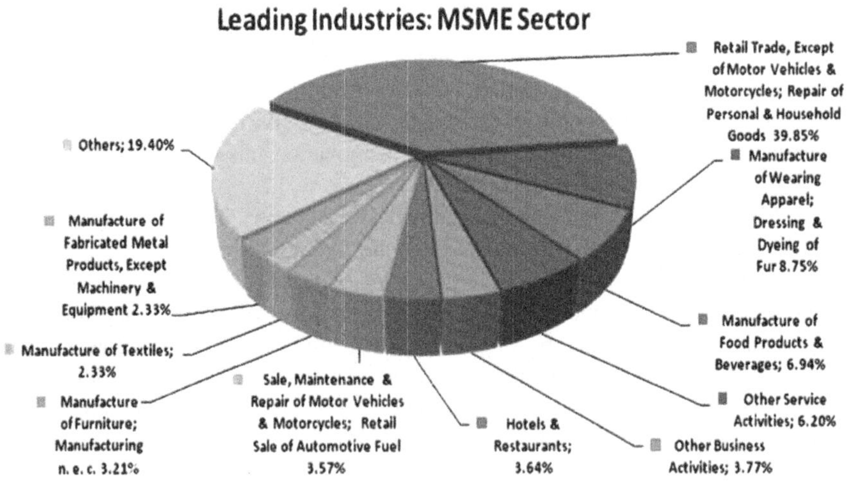

Fig. 1.1 Share of different leading Indian MSMEs *Source* Annual reports 2012-13, Govt. of India, MSME

1.5 Background for the Study

However, the contribution of MSMEs to GDP, manufacturing output and export has been reported declining in the past few years. MSMEs, as individual and collective entities, are not as robust as the large enterprises to deal with the economic, social or functional issues. Such complex and unfriendly ecosystem has forced the MSMEs to enter into an informal and unorganized segment. As a result, the unregistered sector is growing at a rate five times faster than the registered sector, and is already about 95% of the total sector. But this trend needs to be checked, as enterprises cannot last long in this way. Though MSMEs are major contributors for the growing Indian economy, they are facing ample number of problems which needs to be addressed immediately. In order to achieve success and acquire the competitive advantage, MSMEs needs strategic marketing rather than the conventional marketing tactics. Strategic marketing is an absolute life saver for the current Indian MSMEs, since it addresses almost all the present issues. This creates a situation where in MSMEs start looking towards strategic marketing rather the conventional marketing.

Strategic marketing essentially looks at innovation. Since the primary aim of this book is to highlight the need for strategic marketing and innovation for MSMEs. In order to do this, we consider MSMEs from Karnataka and Tamil Nadu which are clustered in and around Bangalore and Coimbatore, since they represent the important industrial belts.

1.6 Objectives of the Study

- Building the measures of Strategic Marketing and Innovation and develop a conceptual research framework for examining the relationship between them.
- Designing a measuring instrument using Strategic Marketing and Innovation measures and test the instrument.
- Examine the relationship between Strategic Marketing and Innovation and also its impact on each.
- Examine the effect of different dimensions of Innovation on Strategic Marketing dimensions and find which of these needs more thrust in an organization.
- Make appropriate suggestions on the need for adoption of SM as a means for any Indian manufacturing organizations to achieve a higher growth rate.

1.7 Imperative Need

MSMEs in order to survive in this ever changing and competitive environment and gain competitive advantage should go in for innovation and strategic marketing. These are discussed in Chaps. 2 and 3.

1.8 Review Questions

1. Elaborate on the evolution of SSIs to MSMEs.
2. Explain the Government policies towards SSIs in India.
3. Define MSMEs. Explain in detail regarding its formation and how it is helping in the development of a nation's economy.

References

Annual Report 2008–09 Ministry of Micro, Small and Medium Enterprises

Economic Survey Report 2009–2010

Annual Report 2008–2009 Ministry of MSME

Report on MSME Third Census 2001–02

Ministry of Micro, Small and Medium Enterprises. Annual Report 2010–2011

Rothwell R (1991) External networking and innovation in small and medium-sized manufacturing firms. Technovation 11(2):93–112

Brenner R (1987) Rivalry in business, science, among nations. Cambridge University Press, Cambridge

Hausman A (2005) Innovativeness among small businesses: theory and propositions for future research. Ind Mark Manage 34(8):773–782

Lall S (1992) Technological capabilities and industrialization. World Dev 20(2):165–186

Lall S 2000 The technological structure and performance of developing country manufactured exports, 1985–1998. Queen Elizabeth House Working Paper Series 44, University of Oxford

Chapter 2
MSMEs-Innovation

Abstract The economic growth of Indian MSMEs is catalysing them into a growing power centre at both local and global market levels. This makes it imperative for them to adopt innovation at all levels. Innovation and entrepreneurship acts as a two sides of a same coin, but differs across the firms only in terms of its scope and magnitude. Today's Indian MSMEs are facing several challenges both internally and externally as a result of dynamic changes happening across the country and also in the rest of the world. To get through such market upheavals, MSMEs need to adopt several strategic initiatives and innovation may be one among them. With the present scenario of liberalization, privatisation and globalisation, it calls for the Indian MSMEs to adopt the culture of innovation at all levels of its operation.

The key takeaways for the reader from this chapter are listed below:

- Innovation in MSMEs: Theory and Trends
- Need for innovation for Indian MSMEs
- India's stand in Global Innovation Index
- Objectives of carrying out innovation by Indian MSMEs

Keywords Innovation · Henderson-Clark framework · Incremental innovation · Architectural innovation · Radical innovation · Global innovation index

2.1 Background

Expected profitable growth is not achieved by Indian MSMEs as a result of huge competition and other challenges and issues that they are facing. Based on the existing statistics and extensive studies done with reference to Indian firms, we could raise a question that "why some of the firms are able to achieve remarkable growth in spite of huge competitive environment"? The answer to this question is "innovation", which we are trying to figure out that is going to make a difference between a low performing company and high performing company.

R. Srinivasan and C.P. Lohith, *Strategic Marketing and Innovation for Indian MSMEs*, India Studies in Business and Economics,
DOI 10.1007/978-981-10-3590-6_2

Actually low performers follow the conventional and good old methodologies to reach the goal. At the same time, high performers are adopting turnaround strategies to achieve the goal and take the benefit of competitive advantage. Low performers are able to gain the momentum of success over a long period of time and many times they may not be successful. High performers are successful and able to reap returns. Usually they will be finding a niche market and enhance their market horizon which is a dream come true for the low performers. Strategic moves adopted by the high performers is adopting the logic of innovation at all levels of its operation starting from identification of customers needs and realization of a product to catch the buzzword of success.

2.2 Imperatives for Innovations

As a result of liberalization, privatization and globalization, MSME sector to emerge as innovative needs to adopt six generic forces and they can act like a catalyst in its growth process.

They are:

(1) Power of Customer
(2) Power of Information
(3) Power of Global investors
(4) Power of market place
(5) Power of simplicity
(6) Power of the organization.

Power of Customer—Today's market is driven by customers. Customer needs to be treated like a king- it is not just satisfying his needs, rather delighting by meeting both his needs and wants. The very reason for this scenario is that the present day customers are aware of what they want. So Indian MSMEs should clearly understand the power of a customer and develop the products or offer services as and when needed. Effort should be to meet their intrinsic and extrinsic needs.

Power of Information—Twenty first century is the era of knowledge and information. Both have to be harnessed to get the required success. Out of these, information has got a big role in the success of any business. The success factor lies directly with the level of information gathered at all levels of its operation and used at the right time. Developing the required product at the time when it is actually needed depends on the information gathered from the market place. Indian MSMEs need to cater to all types of information available across the globe and take strategic decision/s to obtain competitive advantage.

Power of Global investors'—Small firms can not only cater to the local needs but also can be a significant player as a global partner with big firms. This is possible as a result of several innovative approaches they have adopted. If some big multinational company is considering a small firm as a vendor, it is evident that small firms have a role to play in their success. So the power of global investor is very critical and needed for the overall growth of both.

Power of the global market place—Today's world is shrinking day by day. As a result of this, it has really become a small village and all the firms are playing in the same market place. An MSME firm which was earlier catering only to the local needs is now entering into global platform and its market space has enormously grown to the global market place. Darwin's theory of survival is very true with respect to these firms as well. If MSMEs of any country has to survive, they need to concentrate on entering into global market by offering innovative and quality products.

Power of simplicity—there is a saying "small is beautiful", and we can similarly quote "simple is difficult". It is very easy to develop a complicated system and at the same time, it is difficult to make things simpler. The real sense of simplicity is the level of efforts and methodical procedures or standards adopted to achieve the simplicity and also at the earliest to enter the market place. Indian MSMEs needs to adopt the same strategy to achieve both short range and long range goals. At the same time, customers also prefer to go with the simple products rather a complicated one.

Power of organization—Success does not come only due to an individual's effort in an organization. It is due to the synergetic effort put forth by each and every individual of different departments across the firm. Any firm can achieve the success if all the people working in the organization believes in team work and its benefits. Indian MSMEs should also realize the strengths, weakness, opportunities and threats that they are going to have and face in order to gain the competitive advantage.

2.3 Innovation in MSMEs: Theory and Trends

Innovation is the most discussed topic in today's competitive world. Researchers have demonstrated various determinants of innovation and the case studies done on innovative firm's states that these firms are following specific variables of innovation and they are the real factors for its success (Fagerberg and Verspagen 2009; Gopalakrishnan and Damanpour 1994). Majority of the studies done on innovative firms predicts a linear model of innovation. As per this study, the originated research findings from the laboratories are transferred to the firms as commercial products/services and from there it reaches the customer the end user (Godin 2006).

Schumpeter (1934) says that innovation is happening as a result of combining several existing inputs and resulting in value addition. He calls this process as a creative destruction. Lall (1992) demonstrates that innovation is a result of adding values to the existing products or its improvement or may be a newer one to meet the customer needs and wants. OECD definition of innovation is characterized by either a new product development or process and it is popularly termed as Technological Product and Process (TPP) innovation (OECD 1996).

According to Dosi (1988) "Innovation is a process of discovering things through several experiments or developing a product may be by just adopting something new through improving the organizational set-ups or its process". Innovation should always result in tangible products/services (Amabile 1988) by making use of technology, marketing and other essentials of new product development. There is substantial evidence that small firms are adopting innovation to a large extent and are able to gain competitive advantage in the global market (Subrahmanya 2005; Edwards et al. 2005; Gopalakrishnan and Damanpour 1994).

MSMEs gain competitive advantage by adopting innovation, which is not a onetime affair rather a continuous process. (Bessant and Caffyn 1997). It is a true fact that any firm will be competitive, if it is innovative (Acs et al. 1994). Eisdorfer and Hsu (2011) say that any firm failing to adopt innovation is falling down the hill and it will be ruined like a bankruptcy. Innovation is an application part of invention and it actually needs the methods of diffusing the invention as a commercial product into the market (Dosi 1988). So any firm has to diffuse the innovation in the form of successful products. Available literature on firms adopting innovation says that, there exists various types of innovation such as product innovation (Ettlie and Bridges 1982), process innovation (Gallouj and Weinstein 1997), incremental innovation (Damanpour 1991), and radical innovation (Duchesneau et al. 1979). The firm adopting a definite type of innovation depends on the level of profit and returns it is expecting and also the firm needs to adopt a continuous innovation as a culture to sustain a steady growth (Škerlavaj et al. 2007). Performance of a firm is directly based on the level of adoption of innovation on a continuous basis (Gunday et al. 2011). The basic need of any firm to be innovative is to cater to the customer requirements and there by expand its market space. Today's MSMEs are actually driven hard to develop large number of variants, since customer requirements are volatile in nature. This has prompted the MSMEs to innovate drastically or else they will be perished (Pirmoradi et al. 2014).

The term "innovation" has been used in three different contexts (Zaltman et al. 1973). First, the term is considered to be synonymous with invention. Second, the term may be synonymous with a new idea. Third, innovation can also be used to describe the process whereby new ideas are accepted, developed and implemented. The last definition recognizes that innovation is a multistage process that occurs over time.

A number of researchers define innovation as any idea, practice or object that the adopting individual or organization regards as new (Damanpour and Evan 1984; Damanpour 1991). Nohria and Gulati (1996) define innovation "very broadly to include any policy, structure, method or process, product or product opportunity that the manager of the innovating unit perceived to be new." According to Van de Ven, "Few innovations make a revolutionary changes and obsolete all the existing technologies and methodologies to emerge an innovative product which is widely acceptable. The rest of the innovations are happening through small modifications as and when needed." Regardless of the definition used to identify organizational behaviours that constitute innovation, researchers in the area widely agree that innovation comes in many forms (Gopalakrishnan and Damanpour 1992; Utterback 1994). These include radical and incremental innovation, technological and administrative innovation, product innovation and process innovation (Utterback and Abernathy 1975). Micro and Macro levels of innovations are the two different levels which an organization can categorize (Damanpour 1991; Kanter 1988). Micro level innovations includes individuals characteristics such as creativity, problem solving and decision making activities, where as Macro level of innovation include system characteristics such as firms capacity and capability to innovate. Further, new dimensions are being looked into by researchers like Richtner and Rognes (2008). Innovation may be understood as either an incremental improvement over the existing techniques/devices or a brand new idea, method, product or device.

Innovation should not remain only as a statement rather it should be a practice on a continuous basis so as to survive itself over a long period and at the same time retain its customer preferences. This happens as a result of interfacing of invention, innovation and diffusion (Dosi 1988). The need for large number of variants across the products/services is increasing over a period of time as a result of ever changing customer's preferences (Pirmoradi et al. 2014) and as well as by the regulations of governments. This has made MSMEs to develop a series of products which caters to the large market space and develop a habit of introducing a family of products catering into several niche markets (Pirmoradi et al. 2014). Product modularity is one of the initiatives made by several innovative firms to meet the demand (Mikkola and Gassmann 2003). Customer demands can be met only through innovative approaches rather than the conventional one. MSMEs are adopting platform based products to cater to the ever increasing demands of the customer.

2.4 The Henderson-Clark Framework of Innovation for MSMEs

The Henderson-Clark (Henderson and Clark 1990) framework can be a framework which any MSME can adopt. On the basis of technological novelty and novelty of linkages that integrates several related components, innovation can be categorized as:

1. Incremental innovation—results in small changes in both form and function.
2. Modular innovation—remarkable changes in function due to rapid changes in technology and having small or no changes in the form.
3. Architectural innovation—drastic changes in form with little changes in function.
4. Radical Innovation—both form and function undergo surgery.

Table 2.1 Henderson and Clark framework for product market strategies

Product-market characteristics	Adopted strategies	Action framework
Existing product × existing market	Market penetration	(i) Increased volume sales per existing users (ii) Advertisements, loyalty schemes, sales promotions, personal selling to existing customers (iii) Increase volume sales by acquiring new users (iv) Market consolidation, mergers and acquisitions (v) Competitive pricing, discounting
New product × existing market	Product development	(i) Enhanced R&D efforts and innovation (ii) Developing insights into customers's needs (iii) First movers in a product category (iv) Increase the overall efficiency of the users
Existing product × new market	Market development	(i) Modify existing product to have new usage for new set of customers (ii) Highlighting new dimensions/packaging of products (iii) New geographical expansion—exports (iv) New distribution channel (v) Market segmentation—new pricing policies
New product × new market	Diversification	(i) New product in new markets (ii) New technology, new skills (iii) New merchandizing, new facilities (iv) New financial investments, new financing models (v) High risk-high rewards

Source Henderson and Clark (1990)

Modular and radical innovations require huge investments, since it concentrates on function rather than on form. As a result, R&D expenses will be significantly high to improve the functional aspects. The following table is the Henderson and Clark framework which indicates the different product market strategies adopted at different levels (Table 2.1).

2.5 Need of Innovation for Indian MSMEs

Indian MSMEs needs to grow beyond the country or continental needs. It should concentrate on entering into global market and thus give a tough competition to the big giants in the market. A recent study done by FICCI (Federation of Indian Chambers of Commerce and Industry) and Centre of Management studies of IIFT (Indian Institute of Foreign Trade) says that there is a high alarm for Indian MSMEs to gain the higher Global Innovation Index (GII) as compared with the countries like China, Singapore, Malaysia, Japan, South Korea etc., which already got higher Global Innovation Index.

In spite of high growth rate, Indian MSMEs are facing several challenges like lack of technology and funding support, huge competition, changes in policies etc.

To survive, MSMEs has to be innovative to go against the conventional wind and make its existence in the competitive world. Hence MSMEs needs to crunch the knowledge and information which is available in plenty and make use of the required item to develop an innovative product and sustain its growth over a long period. MSMEs have to improve its performance by making use of right set of knowledge and information and drive the economy. Innovation is an answer to drive this knowledge based economy and it can be leveraged to the maximum extent to gain the competitive advantage. Innovation should be used as a weapon by both developed and developing countries effectively to enhance their firm's performance and make their firm competitive in the global market.

As a result of higher potential with respect to employment and growth, MSMEs is an answer next to large industries. Indian government has already taken several strategic steps to see that MSMEs are able achieve the targets by adopting these innovative initiatives. According to a National knowledge commission of India's study, 17% of the MSMEs are in the pipeline of introducing new products into the market. The commission also say that the thrust area for enhancing the competitiveness is Technology, skill development and innovation. Innovation has been due importance since it is much of about execution and it's all about the creative ideas incorporated to produce an economically viable products. Indian firms are now aiming to achieve the success through innovation or else they know that they will be perished by the competitors.

Indian MSMEs needs to adopt several of the new innovative thoughts and ideas so as to make a revolutionary change among the players across the globe. Such revolutionary change which was brought out by an Indian automobile giant Tata Motors and it's none other than a NANO car. Indian MSMEs are now catering into several sectors such as manufacturing, IT services, medicine, health care, education, telecommunication and so on. But still Indian MSMEs are having high potential to enter into several niche markets and gain the competitive advantage.

2.6 India's Stand in Global Innovation Index

Innovation is still a nightmare as far as Indian companies are concerned since most of them know less about the impact of innovative products/service that happen in the market. They are less aware of the level of innovation and the type of diffusion happening. Global Innovation Index (GII) is such an index which helps any country to benchmark their status as with respect to innovations are concerned.

The GII, therefore, aims at establishing the following key facets:

1. It instigates policy makers to highlight the importance of innovation or otherwise difficult to find its relevance.
2. It frames guidelines to revaluate the process of innovation.
3. It will be a measuring tool to evaluate the firms which are innovative at the national level.

The following are the status of India's GII:

- India is ranked 62nd on the GII, 1st in its region, and 8th in its income group—after China, Moldova, Jordan, Thailand, Viet Nam, Ukraine, and Guyana.
- India is the second most densely populated country, with 1.2 billion inhabitants.
- It is eleventh in GDP, with US$1,310 billion.
- A lower-middle-income country, it comes second after Sri Lanka in GDP per capita in PPP dollars in the region.
- India comes in at 44th on the Output Sub-Index.
- Within the top 30 on labour productivity growth (21st with 4.5%) and computer and communications services exports (4th globally, with 70.0% of total commercial service exports).
- It also has positions within the top 40 on two knowledge diffusion indicators: high-tech exports.
- (32nd, at 6.34% of GDP) and FDI net out-f lows (38th, at 1.08% of GDP).
- On pillar 6, Creative outputs, it ranks 39th on national feature films produced, 22nd on daily newspapers, 9th on creative goods exports, and 29th on creative services exports.
- India's position, however, is dragged down by its poor performance on the Input side (ranked 87th): India is in the last quintile on sub-pillars business environment, elementary education, tertiary education, and knowledge workers.
- But the country has high marks—within the top 40—on R&D (35th); general infrastructure (11th).

2.7 Objectives of Carrying Out Innovation by Indian MSMEs

- To produce quality products.
- To upgrade the existing technology to the newer one.
- To optimize the manufacturing cost.
- To optimize investment on resources.
- To enhance product variants.
- To improve product life cycle time.
- To increase market space.
- To promote agility in manufacturing.
- To seek for niche markets.
- To follow domestic regulation
- To minimize the impact of industrialization on environment.
- To enhance the comfort level of employees by providing good infrastructural facilities.

2.8 Review Questions

1. Explain the need of innovations for Indian MSMEs.
2. Explain the Henderson-Clark framework of innovation for Indian MSMEs.
3. Explain India's stand on global innovation index.
4. Elaborate on the objectives of carrying out innovation by Indian MSMEs.

References

Acs et al (1994) R&D spillovers and recepient firm size. Rev Econ Stat 76:336–340
Amabile T (1988) A model of creativity and innovation in organization. Res Organ Behav 10:123–167
Bessant and Caffyn (1997) Rediscovering continuous improvement. Technovation 14(1):17–29
Damanpour F (1991) Organizational innovation: a meta-analysis of effects of determinants and moderators. Acad Manag J 34(2):555–590
Damanpour and Evan (1984) Organizational innovation and performance: the problem of organizational lag. Admin Sci Quart 29:392–409
Dosi G (1988) Sources, procedures and microeconomic effects of innovation. J Econ Lit 26 (3):1120–1171
Duchesneau et al. (1979) A Study of Innovation in Manufacturing: Determinants, Processes and Methodological Issues. Soc Sci Res Foundation, University of Maine, Orono, ME
Edwards et al. (2005) Understanding innovation in small and medium-sized enterprises: a process manifest. Technovation 25(10):1119–1127
Eisdorfer and Hsu (2011) Innovate to Survive: The Effect of Technology Competition on Corporate Bankruptcy. 40(4):1087–1117
Ettlie JE, Bridges WP (1982). Environmental Uncertainty and Organizational Technology Policy. IEEE Trans Engg Manage (1):2–10
Fagerberg J, Verspagen B (2009) Innovation studies-the emerging structure of a new scientific field. Res Policy 38(2):218–233
Gallouj F, Weinstein O (1997) Innovation in Services. Res Policy 26(4–5):537–556
Godin B (2006) The linear model of innovation: the historical construction of an analytical framework. Sci Technol Human Values 31(6):631–667
Gopalakrishnan and Damanpour (1992) Innovation research in economics, sociology, and technology management: a review and synthesis. P Aca Manage 52:488
Gopalakrishnan S, Damanpour F (1994) Patterns of generation and adoption of innovation in organizations: contingency models of innovation attributes. J Eng Tech Manage 11:95–116
Gunday et al (2011) Effects of innovation types on firm performance. Int J Prod Economics 662:676–713
Henderson RM, Clark KB (1990) Architectural innovation: the reconfiguration of existing product technologies and the failure of established firms. Admin Sci Quart 35(1):9–31
Kanter RM (1988) When a thousand flowers bloom: Structural, collective, and social conditions for innovation in organizations. Res Organ Behav (10):169–211
Lall S (1992) Technological capabilities and industrialization. World Dev 20(2):165–186
Mikkola JH, Gassmann O (2003) Managing Modularity of Product Architectures: Toward an Integrated Theory. IEEE Trans on Engg Manage 50(2):204–217
Nohria and Gulati (1996) Is slack good or bad for innovation? Acad Manag J 39(5):1245–1264
Pirmoradi et al. (2014) A Review of Recent Literature in Product Family Design and Platform-Based Product Development, New York, Heidelberg, Dordrecht, London: Springer 1–46

OECD (1996) The measurement of scientific and technological activities: proposed guidelines for collecting and interpreting technological innovation data- oslo manual, 2nd edn. OECD, Paris
Richtner and Rognes (2008) Organizing R&D in a global environment: Increasing dispersed co-operation versus continuous centralization. Eur J Innovation Manage 11(1):125–141
Schumpeter Joseph A (1934) The theory of economic development. Harvard University Press, Cambridge MA
Subrahmanya MH (2005) Small scale industries in india in the globalization era: performance and prospects. Int J Manage Enterp Dev 2(1):122–139
Utterback JM (1994) Mastering the dynamics of innovation: How companies can seize opportunities in the face of technological change. Boston: Harvard Business School Press
Utterback JM, Abernathy WJ (1975) A dynamic model of process and product innovation, Omega (3):639–656
Zaltman et.al. (1973) Innovations and organizations. New York: Wiley

Chapter 3
MSMEs-Strategic Marketing

Abstract Strategic marketing plan adopted by most of the Indian MSMEs do not go beyond the formulation of mission-vision statements. Most of the time, this move will not help the firm to obtain the expected success. An effective strategic plan needs a MSME to have an action plan covering long-term objectives derived from its mission-vision statements. In spite of knowing the importance of strategic marketing, most of the Indian organizations devote less time towards implementing this at the organizational levels. It is very high time that now this can be practically implemented to see the drastic improvement. Planning for strategic marketing will definitely result in rapid changes which yields a huge success for any MSME.

The key takeaways for the reader from this chapter are listed below

- Strategic marketing in MSMEs: Theory and Trends
- Need of Strategic marketing for Indian MSMEs
- Objectives of carrying out Strategic marketing by Indian MSMEs

Keywords Strategic marketing · New products · Firm performance · Marketing mix · Customer relationship management · Competitive advantage

3.1 Background

Any firm's growth and its existence depend highly on its capability to develop and market a product of its own. This makes any firm to realize the importance of new product development by utilizing all its resources to maximize its returns (Day 1994; McEvily et al. 2004; Nerkar and Roberts 2004; Sorescu et al. 2003). Necessarily, a firm needs to have good resources as far as technology and marketing are concerned. These need to be put together to develop a new product which leads to success through market exploitation (Sirmon et al. 2007).

Superior innovation capability is a key contributor to firm performance. The capacity to innovate can assist firms in the process of developing superior products

R. Srinivasan and C.P. Lohith, *Strategic Marketing and Innovation for Indian MSMEs*, India Studies in Business and Economics,
DOI 10.1007/978-981-10-3590-6_3

to meet their customers' changing needs and demands (Verhees and Meulenberg 2004; Li and Mitchell 2009; Rosenbusch et al. 2011) which is a requirement to succeed in the marketplace. Furthermore, firms must also possess superior marketing capability to bring their products to the marketplace faster and serve the customers better than their rivals (Vorhies and Morgan 2005; O'Dwyer et al. 2009).

Marketing concept is understood well over a period of time (Drucker 1994). Its operations have become somewhat difficult since the concept falls into an organizational philosophy rather than a strategic tool. Researchers like Gronroos (1990) and Gummesson (1987) believe that in a broader sense marketing has to take care of total customer relationship for successful marketing. As per the view of several researchers in the field of marketing, they argue that marketing strategy has to be initiated based on the segmentation, targeting and positioning (STP) model (Kotler 2005; Walker et al. 2001; Perreault and McCarthy 2002).

Kotler (2005) demonstrates that marketing strategy is all about how a firm specifically targets a customer by proper usage of marketing mix and able to target them through proper positioning. In this context, it demands innovative marketing tools to be used as required appropriately. The relevance of marketing strategy is properly judged by evaluating the difference of opinion between the customer's perception and the offerings made by a firm (Perreault and McCarthy 2002).

Both emerging global production and knowledge networks needs to be understood by any small enterprise which enables it to compete in the present day's age of liberalization and globalization (Basant et al. 2010). Definitely this has been realized by the key policy makers to take note of small sectors while framing guidelines and policies, since they play a major role. Any Indian small enterprise adopting an effective strategic marketing will definitely yield good result and contributes to the overall development of its economic growth.

3.2 Strategic Marketing in Indian MSMEs: Theory and Trends

Most suitable approach for an Indian MSME is well explained by Henry Mint Berg's observation of strategic planning as an oxymoron (Fanersher 2003). Few of the Indian firms adopt an effective strategic planning that go beyond mission-vision statements. Rest of the firms do not think about framing long term objectives which otherwise should have been. These firms need to be serious about the implementation of the strategic initiatives taken to achieve the sustained growth. This needs to be thought in terms of out of the box thinking (Friedman 2000; Gootee 1998).

Strategic marketing is formulated at different stages of a firm's growth. For example, both product line width and depth can be increased to enhance the effect of market mix (Kotler and Keller 2008).Market mix as a marketing strategy is considered to be a significant factor which influences the small firm's performance (Romano and Ratnatunga 1995).

MSMEs can gain competitive advantage only through adopting an effective strategic marketing (Yen and Chew 2011). The importance of strategic marketing, 4Ps and market intelligence system along with networking as an additional tool of marketing can surely benefit small enterprises (Gilmore et al. 2001). Kwaku and Satyendra Singh (1998) demonstrated the importance of customer oriented approach for MSME products.

Strategic marketing is a tool used by a firm to achieve excellence and it mainly deals with product pricing, selling and its distribution. Any small business unit can achieve higher growth by using this as a strategy and it can enhance its market share by developing new products to both existing and future markets (Srinivasan 2014).

Marketing strategies need arises as a result of filling the gap between the customer perception of a product/service and the market offerings from a firm. Richardson et al. argue more the customer able to understand about the market offerings from a firm through 4Ps, more is the level of marketing strategies adopted.

Strategic marketing deals mainly with marketing aspects of a firm with long term implications. Nowadays, small firms have gained the capabilities of predicting the future trends and this has really helped them to take decisions at all levels to gain competitive advantage. With this capability, these firms can really exploit the market to a greater extent and achieve the success (Anderson 1999). Indian MSMEs needs to adopt this type of strategy to achieve the growth at a faster rate.

3.3 Need of Strategic Marketing for Indian MSMEs

The MSMEs cannot generate revenue by selling same old products to the same old market in the same old way. Almost all firms under MSME sector are in highly volatile market and facing cut throat competition. A few among them are able to sustain themselves and able to sail through using strategic marketing. To make strategic marketing technique to work, it needs to have proper strategic planning with a 100% commitment from all the personnel in the organization. Persons at the decision making level need to consider various innovative marketing tools and adopt few or many on the basis of their workability.

Indian MSMEs business environment has been drastically disturbed by the huge competition and ever changing customer demands in the market. In order to understand the steps taken or adopted by these firms, one need to understand what is the practical measures adopted by these firms to combat against the challenges and threats that they are facing. In short, what is the strategy they are adopting for this paradigm shift? This can provide insight into how Indian MSMEs are considering taking necessary initiatives to face the global challenges.

There are many innovative marketing techniques, which can be considered by the managers for their enterprises. The most popular and usable tools for the MSMEs for their product marketing are given below:

1. WWW as a Promotional Tool
2. Customer Relationship Management (CRM)
3. Digital Advertising
4. Mobile applications as a Service tool
5. Improving feedback mechanism
6. Following up leads and convert it in sales
7. Generate new sparks (Idea)
8. Cluster Approach

The Strategic marketing can function effectively only when there exists an equal involvement from both employees and the management of a firm. MSMEs can definitely implement these strategies since they are flexible in nature as far as decision aspects are concerned. This will result in making MSMEs to formulate a strategic plan to achieve the goal through effective marketing strategies. These innovative strategies will surely help MSMEs to realize their potential in acquiring the market share.

3.4 Objectives of Carrying Out Strategic Marketing by Indian MSMEs

The marketing departments of all the firms who take care of customer perception has to gear up further and understand what is the reality as far as the changing scenario is concerned. Thus our present work is about how strategic marketing can emerge as a tool to achieve success in a short span for Indian MSMEs. The specific objectives are, as stated below.

1. To identify several constructs under strategic marketing and find their significance with respect to the MSMEs innovation performance.
2. To suggest which of the identified constructs under strategic marketing has got greater role in achieving competitive advantage for the firm.

3.5 Review Questions

1. What is strategic marketing? Explain its implication on Indian MSMEs.
2. Explain the need of strategic marketing for Indian MSMEs.
3. Explain the objectives of carrying out strategic marketing practices by Indian MSMEs.

References

Anderson M (1999) Why diversity professionals should care about SMEs. J HRM 16(4):67–71
Basant et al (2010) "Arrested Virtual Cycle? Higher Education and High-technology Industries in India" in Annual World Bank Conference on Development Economics 2009, Global: People, Politics, and Globalization ed. Justin Yifu Lin and Boris Pleskovic. Washington, DC: World Bank, 2010.
Day G (1994) The capabilities of market-driven organizations. J Mark 58(4):37–52.
Drucker PF (1994) Innovation and entrepreneurship: practice and principles. Heinemann, London
Friedman S (2000) Work place arrangement strategy. J pers manag 12(3):12–15
Fanersher J (2003) Strategies enhanced by corporate. J Manag 34(8):30–33
Gootee BH (1998) Flexible work arrangements: managing the work-family boundary. Bus Rev, dt 12(5):2000
Gilmore A, Carson D, Grant K (2001) SME marketing in practice. Mark Intell Plann 19(1):6–11
Gronroos C (1990) Relationship approach to marketing in service contexts: The marketing and organizational behavior interface. J Bus Res 20(1):3–11.
Gummesson E (1987) "The New Marketing –Developing Long-term Interactive Relationships", Long Range Plann 20(4):10–20.
Kotler (2005) Marketing Management, edn. New York: Prentice Hall.
Kotler P, Keller Kl (2008) Marketing management, 12th revised edn. Prentice Hall, Singapore
Kwaku AA, Satyendra S (1998) Customer orientation and performance: a study of SMEs. Manage Decis 36(6):385–394
Li and Mitchell (2009) The Pace and Stability of Small Enterprise Innovation in Highly Dynamic Economies: A China-Based Template, J Small Bus Manage 47(3):370–397.
McEvily SK, Eisenhardt KM, Prescott JE (2004) "The global acquisition, leverage, and protection of technological competencies", Strategic Manage J 25:713–22.
Nerkar A, Roberts PW (2004) Technological and product-market experience and the success of new product introductions in the pharmaceutical industry. Strategic Manage J 25(1):779–799.
O'Dwyer M, Gilmore A, Carson D (2009) Innovative marketing in SMEs: an empirical study, J Strategic Marketing 17(5):383–396.
Perreault and McCarthy (2002) Basic Marketing-A global managerial approach–New Delhi-Tata McGraw Hill.
Romano C, Ratnatunga J (1995) The role of marketing: its impact on small enterprise research.In Conference proceedings: research at the marketing/entrepreneurship interface, University of Illinois at Chicago, Chicago, IL, 111–136
Rosenbusch N, Brinckmann J, Bausch A (2011) Is innovation always beneficial? A meta-analysis of the relationship between innovation and performance in SMEs, J Bus Venturing 26:441–457.
Sirmon et al (2007) Managing firm resources in dynamic environments to create value: looking inside the black box. Acad Manage Rev 32(1):273–292
Sorescu Alina B, Rajesh K. Chandy, Jaideep C. Prabhu (2003) "Sources and Financial Consequences of Radical Innovation: Insights from Pharmaceuticals," J Marketing 67 (October), 82–101.
Srinivasan R (2014) Strategic management-the indian context‖. Prentice-hall Of India Pvt Ltd
Verhees FJHM, Meulenberg, MTG (2004) Market orientation, innovativeness product innovation, and performance in small firms. J Small Bus Manage 42(2):134–154.
Vorhies DW, Morgan NA (2005) Benchmarking marketing capabilities for sustainable competitive advantage. J Marketing 69(1):80–94.
Walker et al (2001) Adaptive policies, policy analysis and policy making, Eur J Oper Res 128:282–289.
Yen S, Chew DAS (2011) An investigation of marketing strategy, business environment and performance of construction SMEs in China. Afr J Bus Manage 5(6):2396–2405. ISSN 1993-8233

Chapter 4
MSMEs-Addressing Issues

Abstract Indian MSMEs constitute a major part of the entire industrial sectors producing goods and also of exports. They are also able to employ a huge number of peoples next to agriculture and manufacture a good number of products ranging from traditional to high technology based products. Because of their small size and flexibility in decision making they are able to react quickly to the changes in the surrounding environment as they don't have a long chain in decision making but at the same time they suffer from many resource constraints. One of the most significant constraints suffered by MSMEs is the financial constraint. Other constraints include human resource, obsolete technology and challenges in complying with Government regulatory procedures. Generally they serve a narrow market by establishing a close contact with customers. MSME sector in India is highly heterogeneous in terms of the size, variety of products and services, and levels of technology. Keeping in view of the challenges, their diversified nature and important role in manufacturing in India, the current study on manufacturing MSMEs was undertaken with the aim to study emerging patterns in innovation to improve the performance of MSMEs.

The key takeaways for the reader from this chapter are listed below

- MSMEs: past versus present
- Need of MSMEs for Indian economic growth
- Issues faced by MSMEs
- Issues that needs immediate attention.

Keywords Manufacturing · Systemic innovation · Entrepreneur · Harmonized system · Venture capital

4.1 MSMEs: Past Versus Present

Indian economic growth in recent past has been categorized as jobless growth as it has not been able to create enough jobs in proportion to the growth of employable population. At the same time the deficit between India's import and export has

R. Srinivasan and C.P. Lohith, *Strategic Marketing and Innovation for Indian MSMEs*, India Studies in Business and Economics,
DOI 10.1007/978-981-10-3590-6_4

widened to over US$10 billion. One of main reasons for this situation is the stagnation in the country's manufacturing sector. At present share of India's manufacturing sector in GDP is 13–14% which needs to be raised to at least 25% if problem of unemployment and trade deficit have to be dealt with seriously. China is a prime example of how manufacturing can really boost the GDP growth of a country. In 1980 India's GDP per capita of $266 was comparable with China's $307 but at present China's GDP per capita has shot up to $6807 which is 4.5 times higher than India's $1499 and one main reason for this is China's highly vibrant and dynamic manufacturing sector.

Micro Small and Medium Enterprises (MSMEs) in India constitute a major part of industrial manufacturing with 45% of country's manufacturing output and 40% of total exports. They are estimated to employ about 60 million persons in over 26 million units throughout the country and manufacture over 6000 products ranging from traditional to high-tech items. Because of their small size and flexibility in decision making they are able to react quickly to the changes in the surrounding environment as they don't have a long chain in decision making but at the same time they suffer from many resource constraints. One of the most significant constraints suffered by MSMEs is the financial constraint. Other constraints include human resource, obsolete technology and challenges in complying with Government regulatory procedures. Generally they serve a narrow market by establishing a close contact with customers. MSME sector in India is highly heterogeneous in terms of the size, variety of products and services, and levels of technology. Keeping in view of the challenges, their diversified nature and important role in manufacturing in India, the current study on manufacturing MSMEs was undertaken with the aim to study emerging patterns in innovation.

4.2 Need of MSMEs for Indian Economic Growth

Available statistics related to the contribution of MSMEs towards India's exports shows a decline from 46.2% in 2009–10 to 43% in 2012–13. This is an alarm for MSMEs to open up themselves and take appropriate strategic decision to avoid further downfall. The reason found out by the Confederation of Indian Industry (CII) was that the MSMEs are not able to market their products/services, lack of infrastructure and funding, lack of R&D and innovation. This calls for Indian MSMEs to adopt innovative approaches to steady their export contribution. Indian MSMEs should make efforts to overcome all the deficiencies identified by CII and increase their market share by entering global market.

As far as exports are concerned Indian MSMEs lag behind MSMEs belonging to several countries like Europe, China, South Korea, Taiwan and Malaysia. For the past several decades Indian MSMEs are exporting products such as readymade garments, leather goods, processed foods, engineering items and sports goods. These products have captured a good share in the global market, but still a lot more remains to be done in the coming days. The major global markets for Indian products from 2009 to 2012 were US, Europe, Turkey, Singapore, Hong Kong, Israel and Saudi Arabia accounting for about 90% of exports through MSMEs. There is still a wide space for Indian MSMEs to increase its global market covering the remaining parts of the world. At the same time, Indian MSMEs need to gear up to meet global standards. Several initiatives need to be taken by government to see that MSMEs which are export-worthy are supported extensively to gain global market share. This will encourage Indian entrepreneurs to exhibit their innovative products/services in the global market and gain competitive advantage.

4.3 Inspiring Innovation in India's MSMEs

One of the co-founders of Intel, Dr. Robert Noyce once said; "**Don't be encumbered by history. Go off and do something wonderful**". This simple philosophy has stuck with Intel for decades and even today, it motivates Intel employees to break the mould, take appropriate risks and push the boundaries in everything they do.

The Culture of Innovation

An essential part of any MSMEs is to create and nurture "the Culture of Innovation", where they can adopt internal processes that encourage and reward engineers to continually push the boundaries in finding new solutions. There are many facets to this but here are a few of the key points:

- **Encourage informed "risk taking"**

Any MSME should rate "risk taking" high in order to elevate its position to the higher level. This should be the core value for any organization which also includes "discipline" and "customer orientation". Nowadays organizations are strictly adhering to its strategic goals along with the informed risk taking among its employees.

- **"Fail early and fail cheap"**

This can be read as part of the risk taking value and encourages employees to test the viability of new ideas as early as possible so they don't waste money during dead ends.

- **Systemic Innovation Engagement Models**

This is a big subject but includes the use of specialized tools designed to lead to breakthrough technologies along with idea "harvesting," where time is set aside to brainstorm on problem solving and moving from ideas to reality.

- **Recognition and reward**

An important part of the culture of innovation is to ensure that they recognize the breakthrough work that gets done so that employees feel properly rewarded and their peers acknowledge them accordingly. This can be done in multiple ways, including inventor recognition when patents are accepted for filing and additional remuneration for patents that are filed in targeted areas.

4.4 Growth Barriers for Our Indian MSMEs

As per existing literature, it is not easy to be an entrepreneur in India. Even in Mumbai which is considered as financial capital of the country it takes 13 procedures and 30 days to start a business while in advanced countries it takes average 4.8 procedures and 9.2 days to start a business. There are a vast number of other formalities which are to be fulfilled before an entrepreneur can really start or to keep a business up and running. Some of these are listed as below:

1. Paying stamp duties online-5 days
2. Filing incorporation documents online-5 days
3. Getting PAN Number-12 days
4. Registering with Employees Provident Fund Organization(EPFO)-12 days
5. Registering with VAT Online-12 days
6. Registering for medical insurance-9 days
7. Getting a Tax Account Number-7 days

Several growth barriers affecting our Indian MSMEs are listed below:

1. Manpower issues
Recently the salary cap to avail Employees' State Insurance (ESI) facilities has been raised from Rs. 15000/-per month to Rs. 25,000 per month. This has increased the number of employees which will be covered under ESI Scheme. This in turn will increase the burden on ESI infrastructure which is already crumbling and also the burden on employers.

There are a huge number of laws dealing with manpower in MSMEs which have only increased corruption and harassment of entrepreneurs at the hands of officials. E.g. there are over 44 central and 100 state labour laws like Industrial Dispute Act-1947, Contract Labour Act-1970, Factories Act-1948 and Apprenticeship Act-1961 containing many archaic and obsolete provisions which need a relook and overhauling. Being an entrepreneur one has to deal with numerous manpower issues like labour unions, strikes, layoffs, work time restrictions for women etc. It is impossible for an entrepreneur to comply with all the provisions laid down in labour laws. Various central agencies carry out approximately 1.75 lakh inspections of MSMEs every year with inspectors having sweeping powers and dealing with them has always been a massive task. All the major trade unions in India are against globalization and see it as anti-labour. Changing their perspective is a huge challenge but it can go a long way in increasing productivity of MSMEs. Another problem which has stagnated the manufacturing in MSMEs is the obstacles presented in the way of big projects due to difficulties in acquiring land and environmental clearances.

2. Problems related with Government R&D departments
While dealing with Govt. R&D departments for technical collaborations and research grants it is observed that there are long delays in getting clearances. Generally there are expert committees to review the feasibility of the proposals but it is observed that there is a need for single committee to review many kinds of proposals.

3. Import/Export Clearances
Classification of good in the * Harmonized System (HS) Codes has been misused to the disadvantage of the indigenous manufacturers. E.g. custom duty may be less for a finished imported product while it may be higher for a component which is supposed to be used by the manufacturer for indigenous manufacturing of the same type of product in the country. This hampers the achievement of self reliance in manufacturing. Many a times there is sudden change in the HS Code of an item creating problems for the firm importing it.

(*Harmonized Commodity Description and Coding System, or the Harmonized System (HS) of tariff nomenclature is an internationally standardized system of names and numbers to classify traded products in order to facilitate import/export of goods among countries.)

4. Threats from China
Chinese goods arriving in India are not tested for safety and other standards compliance while Indian goods are tested thoroughly for such compliance. Another problem arises from large scale import/dumping of items manufactured in China which is available at rock bottom prices. As a result of this many of Indian manufacturers have just turned into traders of Chinese goods. This has set a decline in the country's manufacturing capabilities.

4.5 Barriers to Innovation Aspects of Indian MSMEs

- Slow, cumbersome and complex government procedures
- Host of old and archaic laws
- Hostile tax regimes
- Extremely slow processing of patent applications
- Low level of collaboration between MSMEs and Government R&D institutions
- Large scale dumping of Chinese goods at rock bottom prices turning many Indian manufacturers into traders of Chinese goods
- Slow import/export clearances.

4.6 Issues That Need Immediate Attention from the Ministry of MSME

Although there is a long list of issues facing Indian MSMEs, current study brings forth following issues which need immediate attention from policy perspective.

- Promoting in-house R&D in MSMEs
- Increasing role of Venture Capital as a viable source of finance
- Promoting joint R&D between MSMEs and Government R&D institutions
- Skill up-gradation of manpower through training
- Increasing use of financial management software's and electronic security systems
- Involvement of junior level staff in the process of new idea generation
- Making tax regime more flexible and reasonable
- Fewer and simpler Government procedures
- Expediting import-export clearances
- Expediting patent awarding process in Indian Patent Office
- Learning's from best practices followed by the both local and global competitors.

4.7 Review Questions

1. Discuss about the past and present status of Indian MSMEs.
2. Explain the need of development of MSMEs for the growth of Indian economy.
3. Explain the growth barriers for Indian MSMEs.
4. Elaborate on the issues that need immediate attention from the Ministry of MSMEs.

References

Ministry of micro, small & medium enterprises. Annual report 2010–2011

Ministry of micro, small & medium enterprises. Report of the working group on micro, small & medium enterprises (MSMEs) growth for 12th five year plan (2012–2017)

Chapter 5
Research Design

Abstract Innovation is the basis for creating and sustaining competitiveness in the existing complex business systems. Innovation is not only limited to products and services as such but also consist of other categories like system innovation, R&D and Technological innovation, innovation management etc. When planning business strategy, it is necessary to have a proper understanding of innovation and the management process. The crucial link between innovation and Strategic Marketing (SM) therefore, is the long-term and short-term strategies, which integrates the action of today with the vision of tomorrow. Innovation can help organizations to achieve the perceived quality as expected by customer from the offered quality. Investigations are required to find out whether the core concept of Strategic Marketing is linked with innovation performance or not.

The key takeaways for the reader from this chapter are listed below

- Development of constructs for measurement
- Development of the research framework
- Development of measuring instrument

Keywords Business strategy · Innovation performance · Incremental innovation · Make in india · Technological innovation · Product innovation · Process innovation · Innovation management · System innovation · Environmental landscaping · Marketing mix · Brand positioning · Entrepreneurial management

5.1 Need for the Rcsearch

It has been observed that Strategic Marketing (SM) is extremely useful for any manufacturing firm to attain the required growth as against the competitors. It can be seen that it is used as a means where Indian firms can make a difference by

R. Srinivasan and C.P. Lohith, *Strategic Marketing and Innovation for Indian MSMEs*, India Studies in Business and Economics,
DOI 10.1007/978-981-10-3590-6_5

improving on its all aspects related to its performance. Some of the findings from the literature say that the firms are able to attain the higher growth who has adopted Strategic marketing. These strategies are able to make the customer satisfied, but at the same time competition and cost pressures are forcing organizations to invest in innovation and customers are expecting organizations to come out with more innovative products and services. Organizations achieve competitive advantage against competitors when it adopts attributes which are very different from its competition. It's all about firm using it in their day to day business.

The requirement for a company to achieve the competitive advantage is through Innovation and also by adopting Strategic marketing (SM) practices to achieve overall growth. This has become more relevant in India as the after effect of the economic reforms liberalization, privatization, globalization and the consequent adoption of SM practices by Indian organizations. Many organizations and industry associations are also thinking in the lines that innovation is the need of the hour and the focus of SM by the organizations is to shift towards 'achieving excellence through innovation'.

In this context, it is required to connect and justify the correlation between innovation and SM in both Indian manufacturing and service organizations. Indian organizations are more traditional in their approach as far as strategies and innovation is concerned. Post liberalization era was emphasizing the strong need of quality management systems and Indian organizations are at a stage now wherein the focus has to be on 'Strategy with innovation' and hence it is required for organizations to improve their innovation performance. It is in this context that it becomes necessary to investigate on several issues like what is the relationship of Strategic Marketing to innovation performance, or how they are related.

Initial literature survey indicates that not much study has been carried out in the area of SM and innovation as far as Indian organizations are concerned; post the economic liberalization i.e. after 1991. From 1991 onwards due to economic liberalization, foreign direct investment was allowed and a number of multinational organizations invested in India. These organizations created a stiff competition to Indian organizations by providing superior quality products with a variety, all at a competitive price to Indian customers. This also acted as a wake-up call to Indian organizations to provide high quality products. During 1990s and 2000s a good number of Indian organizations had implemented many of the standard practices for achieving quality in their products and services and were capable of providing quality products and services to customers. As the market competition again increased, providing quality products and services alone was not sufficient, but in addition, it was required to provide products with a touch of innovation to attract customers. This demanded innovation in product, process, technology, system and in almost all areas of an organization. These necessitated the firms to consider both strategies and innovation together and derive benefits. In this context, it is required to investigate how these two are related. Though research studies could be traced regarding the relationship of these two with respect to organizations outside India, such studies could not be traced with respect to Indian counterpart.

Innovation is the basis for creating and sustaining competitiveness in the existing complex business systems. Innovation is not only limited to products and services as such but also consist of other categories like system innovation, R&D and Technological innovation, innovation management etc. When planning business strategy, it is necessary to have a proper understanding of innovation and the management process. The crucial link between innovation and SM therefore, is the long-term and short-term strategies, which integrates the action of today with the vision of tomorrow. Innovation can help organizations to achieve the perceived quality as expected by customer from the offered quality. Investigations are required to find out whether the core concept of Strategic Marketing is linked with innovation performance or not.

A number of questions are hovering around as given below, and to investigate further it is required to search for answers for the following questions:

- Whether SM is promoting the innovation performance of Indian organizations?
- How far SM is relevant for management of innovation?
- Is there a relationship existing between SM and innovation?
- If a relationship exists, then which dimension of SM is supporting which category of innovation?
- How can Indian organizations effectively improve innovation performance using SM as a platform?
- Do the SM excellence models involve the measurement of innovation performance?
- Are the shorter life cycles of products forcing organizations to be more innovative? How is this compatible with the SM dimension of continuous improvement?
- What should be the focus—continuous improvement or continuous innovation?
- Whether SM is reinforcing incremental innovation?
- How well is innovation helping organizations to achieve the perceived quality as against the offered quality?
- What are the conflicting accounts of the relationship between SM and innovation?
- Should Indian organizations continue to implement SM as a means in the coming days to achieve competitiveness?
- Can SM function as a specific resource that allows organizations to improve their competence and competitiveness in innovation?
- How the uncertainties in environment affect the innovation for manufacturing organizations?
- Do the various dimensions of SM affect the determinants of business innovation capability?

Organizations need an answer to many of the above questions. Obviously, a research can give an answer to some of the questions mentioned above.

5.2 Gap Identified with Reference to Strategic Marketing and Innovations Adopted by Indian MSMEs

From the available literature, it is very hard to get any research work which has taken strategic marketing and Innovation as the variables considered together with respect to the Indian Micro Small Medium Enterprises under manufacturing sector. Indian MSMEs especially the manufacturing firms are the backbone of our economy which needs to be nurtured well for our nation's benefit. In this context, we found that the research in the field of MSME is the need of the hour. Also our work is in line with the present Indian government's agenda of "Make in India" slogan. The developing country's economy directly relates with the number of small enterprises contribution. With reference to our country's economy, we should see that the environment is very much suitable for any small industries to perform well both locally and as well as in the global context. From the available facts, our Indian MSMEs still has every chance to contribute to the fullest extent.

MSME has become a most promising and highly dictating sector for our Indian economy. Its development is not new for our country, since its conception was the brain child of our Late Prime Minister Jawaharlal Nehru. His vision about MSMEs was its ability to become a backbone for the economic growth of our country. It took several years to sustain in the initial years of its existence. Now there is a speculation about India becoming second country having largest manufacturing firms ahead of US by 2050. The several policies implemented by the Government have made these sectors to achieve sustainable growth and its growth can be further enhanced by giving more importance towards these sectors. Indian MSMEs needs several issues to be addressed in order to meet the present Governments dream of "Make in India" vision. The economy of any developing nation directly depends on the number of entrepreneurs developing innovative products that turnaround the strategic perspective of the organizations and as well the nation's economy. MSMEs in India are presently facing number of problems that needs to be addressed immediately. Those problems are Technology related, scale of operation, logistics, local and global Competition, finance, production techniques, marketing and meeting customer requirements. The answer for these problems can be strategically handled by our MSMEs by adopting innovations in all activities related to day to day operations. Especially the manufacturing firms are really unable to face the tough competition and as a result of this, our economy is not able to meet the targeted growth. Our research is about the literature review done on Indian MSMEs, innovation and strategic marketing interventions needed for overall growth of the firms. The outcome of our research work will be to be show how MSMEs needs to be innovative in the market place and adopt strategic marketing to exceed its excellence against their competitors.

5.3 Proposed Research Work

This has triggered us to develop a framework by taking constructs of Strategic Marketing as independent variables and the constructs of Innovation as dependent variables. We would like to test whether overall performance of a manufacturing firm will be improved as a result of the considering both Strategic marketing and Innovation together. We will be making use of the five different variables Technological Innovation, Product Innovation, Process Innovation, System Innovation and Innovation Management as the dependent variables against constructs of Strategic Marketing such as Environmental Landscaping, Marketing mix, Brand Positioning and Entrepreneurial Management as independent variables in our research. We will be further evaluating all the five models which will be built by taking the effect of strategic marketing on different constructs of innovation performance of manufacturing firms. We will be then able to mention which specific variable is affecting the overall performance of an organization. The gap identified will be addressed in the form a framework which will be an answer for the present day's MSMEs status. So in our research, we are making use of these constructs and it is an attempt to find how Strategic marketing can be used to improve the innovation performance of an Indian MSMEs.

5.4 The Objectives of Research

Literature survey reveals that some studies have been carried out earlier with respect to developing countries other than India. Studies with reference to Indian manufacturing organizations are few and there exists a scope for doing its studies. It is required to narrow down the study to a specific industry or a specific sector. The specific research objectives identified for our work is illustrated below. Objectives have taken into consideration some of the research gaps of previous researchers. Not all the research gaps identified can be addressed in one research. This research basically attempts to study the impact of strategic marketing on innovation performance. It also addresses some of the research gaps, which are relevant and could be analyzed through present research. The research objectives were formulated as per these aspects.

The research is taken up with respect to micro small and medium Indian manufacturing organizations with the following specific objectives.

1. Develop measures of Strategic Marketing and Innovation performance and a research framework for studying the relationship existing between strategic marketing and innovation performance.
2. Develop a measuring instrument using the measures and establish its reliability and validity.
3. Study the relationship existing between Strategic Marketing and Innovation performance within organizations and the impact of Strategic marketing on innovation performance of organizations.

4. Study the impact of different dimensions of Strategic marketing on different types of innovation performance and identify the dimensions of Strategic marketing which require more emphasis within the organization.
5. Make appropriate suggestions on the need for adoption of Strategic marketing as a model in the future, by Indian manufacturing organizations particularly if they want to achieve a high innovation performance.

5.5 Expected Contribution and Possible Direction of Research

This research looks into the impact of Strategic Marketing on the innovation performance of manufacturing organizations. The outcomes of this work give an insight to the organizations as to how far their Strategic Marketing are effective and what is their effect as far as innovation is concerned. The findings of this research could be used by organizations for formulating suitable strategies to improve their competitiveness.

5.6 Research Design Decision

To arrive at a design decision it is required to find answer to certain questions. The typical questions and the corresponding answers for the proposed research are given in Table 5.1. Each one of the items in this table is subsequently discussed in detail.

Table 5.1 Research design questions and answers

Questions for research design decisions	Answers for the proposed research
What is the study about?	Strategic marketing and innovation performance
Why the study is being made?	Innovation, the need of the hour for organizations
Where will the study be carried out?	Manufacturing organizations
What type of data required?	Primary data
Where can be the data available?	Organizations falling under MSME category
What periods will the study include?	Post liberalization in India (after 1991)
What will be the sample design?	Non probability sampling
What are the techniques of data collection?	Questionnaire
How is the data analyzed?	Multivariate statistical techniques
Style of report?	Ex post facto research report

Table 5.2 Factors of research design

Factors	Present research tackles it by
The means of collecting the data	Primary data collection
The skills of the research group	IISc intellect and the industry interaction
Objectives of the problem	Impact of Strategic Marketing on innovation performance
Nature of the problem	Ex post facto study

The factors to be considered in a research design for a particular research problem is given in the Table 5.2.

5.7 Development of Constructs for Measurement

A refined and redefined familiar concept to suit a particular subject is called a construct. It is clear and precise. A construct not directly linked to perception or observation, is termed as theoretical construct (Krishnaswamy et al. 2006).

Considering the literature survey, objectives, organizational visits and conference participations, constructs and items that describe the concepts were developed for making a questionnaire for primary data collection from organizations. The evaluation criteria and studies identify various measures and criteria, for evaluating the strategic marketing and innovation performance within an organization.

An organization can be innovative in many areas, which as per the literature can be in its process, product, R&D and technology, systems and its overall capability of managing the innovation. If it is required to measure the innovation performance in each of these areas its is required to measure the aspects like profitability, time for idea generation to commercialization, funds invested in growth projects, employee strength, R&D effectiveness and efficiency, life cycle performance, customer satisfaction, time to volume and scale, start-up costs, speed etc. Hence measuring the organizations performance in the above aspects with respect to each type of innovation reveals the innovation performance of the organization.

From the studies carried out constructs and items required for Strategic Marketing and innovation were found out. Four constructs have been identified for Strategic Marketing and five constructs have been identified for innovation performance. These constructs are also schematically represented by means of radial diagrams in Figs. 5.1 and 5.2 and these are the variables under strategic marketing and innovation performance which will be measured and evaluated.

5.8 Constructs of Strategic Marketing

See Fig. 5.1.

Fig. 5.1 Identified constructs of strategic marketing

5.9 Constructs of Innovation Performance

See Fig. 5.2.

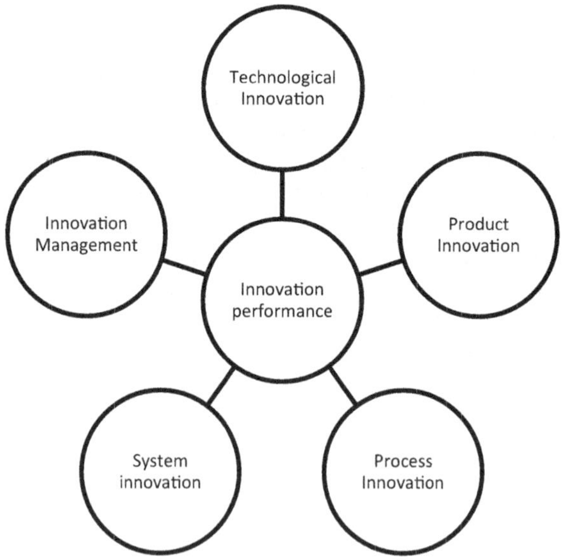

Fig. 5.2 Identified constructs of innovation performance

5.10 Defining the Constructs

The **Environmental Landscaping** construct examines how the organization's senior leaders view customers, competitors, environment factors and other aspects which will lead to profitability. It also investigates the organization's governance and how it addresses its legal, ethical and community responsibilities.

The **Marketing Mix** construct examines how 4Ps (Product, Price, Place, and Promotion) realize the firm's marketing objectives through value added products to its customers. The 4P's are effectively implemented to realize the firm's objectives in the long term.

The **Brand Positioning** construct is defined as the conceptual place you want to own in the targeted consumer's mind—the benefits you want them to think of when they think of your brand. An effective brand positioning strategy will maximize customer relevancy and competitive distinctiveness, in maximizing brand value.

The **Entrepreneurial Management** construct is defined as the creative way of managing the resources for maximising the profitability of the company and as well meets the goals. An effective entrepreneurial management will make the company attain competitive advantage.

The **Technological innovation** construct examines the organizations ability to adapt to new technology, its full utilization, strength of R&D and technological capability acquisition programmes

The **Product innovation** construct examines the novelty of new products, product development capabilities, speed of new product development, organizations leadership in product innovation, ability to respond to customers requirements and early market entry capabilities.

The **Process innovation** construct examines the novelty of new processes, speed of process innovation and capability to develop new processes.

The **System innovation** construct examines the organizations learning capability, proactive approach to innovation, ability to consider innovation as a strategy, adaptability to new ways of organizing, teamwork, cross-functional collaboration, problem solving skills and ability to overcome barriers to creativity.

The **Innovation management** construct examines the organizations innovation management capabilities consisting of top management attitude and commitment to innovation, creative culture and activities to improve the creative potential of its human resources, structure that promotes creativity, resource provision for innovation and association with external agencies involving innovation.

5.11 Questionnaire Development

The research requires collection of primary data from organizations. Primary data is the data specially collected in a research afresh and for the first time and thus happen to be original in character. There are a number of methods available for

Table 5.3 Number of items for each variable

Strategic marketing variables	Items	Innovation variables	Items
Environmental landscaping	12	Technological innovation	10
Marketing mix	12	Product innovation	10
Brand positioning	12	Process innovation	10
Entrepreneurial management	12	System innovation	10
		Innovation management	10
Total	48		50

primary data collection and the questionnaire method is adopted here. Questionnaire is the instrument used for data collection in survey research for large samples. Impersonal and standard format is used in getting data objectively. Information, facts, attitudes, motivation and knowledge are captured easily by questionnaires. Table 5.3 shows the details of the number of items for each variables considered during the questionnaire development.

The questionnaire developed for our work is a structured questionnaire. Adequate attention has been given on the question sequence, formulation and wording, layout etc. to do the survey effectively in order to collect the quality response. The questionnaire is targeted towards senior managers/top managers at the general management level, who are holding key responsibilities in the overall management of the organization with additional responsibilities in strategic marketing management function, or who are well informed about the strategic marketing systems of the manufacturing organization. The objectives of the questionnaire, the methodology of response required etc. are spelt out in the beginning with a request for co-operation.

The first part of the questionnaire starts with the basic information regarding the organization viz. name of organization, products of organization, address, name of senior managers, designation, category of organization, size of organization, Strategic Marketing (SM) initiatives of organization etc.

The second and third parts of the questionnaire measure the SM and innovation performance within the organization respectively. The organization's status on the four SM variables and five innovation performance variables, identified according to the respondents is measured here. A set of statements with respect to the variable under study are given, in which the respondents have to give their level of agreement to the statement with respect to their organization. In the current research, only duly completed questionnaire is collected from the organizations. The respondents are free to discuss the questionnaire with other senior managers of their organization and the feedback or response is considered as the collective voice of the senior managers regarding their organization. Managers at the general management level who are having multifunctional responsibilities (e.g. general manager, management representative etc.) respond the questionnaire. These managers were given specific instructions so that they can make other functional managers also involved for the exercise. The approach for ensuring this was, conveying the matter to the respondents either personally or thru mails. In other words, it has to be mentioned that the feedback given by the senior manager is not an individual perception of the concerned manager but it is the perception of the senior management as a whole regarding their organization.

As mentioned earlier, here the data is collected using the likert Scale. Each variable of SM and innovation are having a number of items ranging from 10 to 12. The response for each item falls in the scale 1–5 as given below:

The respondent who

Strongly agree to a statement gives a score of 5
Just agree to a statement gives a score of 4
Has a neutral opinion i.e. neither agree nor disagree gives a score of 3
Just disagree with the statement gives a score of 2
Strongly disagree with the statement gives a score of 1.

This way the questionnaire has been developed (Annexure-I). The questionnaire measures the SM practices and innovation performance of organizations by means of a set of constructs specifically chosen to measure these variables. The variables of SM and Innovation used for the research almost clearly depict the concepts.

5.12 Review Questions

1. Explain the need for doing applied research and how it is making an impact on the society.
2. Explain research design in detail.
3. What do you mean by constructs and how do you measure it?
4. Elaborate on the use of questionnaire as a measuring instrument used in the research.

Reference

Krishnaswamy KN et al (2006) Management research methodology, 1st edn. Pearson Education

Chapter 6
Pilot Study—Assessment of Validity and Reliability

Abstract A pilot survey is actually the imitation and trail of the main survey. The very purpose of doing a pilot study is to find out any flaw if it exists in the measuring instrument. Questionnaire is the measuring instrument employed in our current study. The responsiveness and applicability of the same has to be ensured through this pilot study by checking the validity and reliability of the questionnaire.

The key takeaways for the reader from this chapter are listed below

- Data collection for pilot study.
- Concept of validity and reliability.

Keywords Questionnaire · Validity · Reliability · Pilot study · Likert scale · Mutitrait multi method matrix · Cronbach alpha

6.1 Data Collection for Pilot Study

During the sampling design stage, we had identified 150 organizations for administering the questionnaire for collecting the data. The criterion for selecting organizations was Micro, Small and Medium scale manufacturing organizations. Earlier discussions were carried out with MSME Department of Institute, Bangalore and Peenya Industrial Association, Bangalore for identifying the organizations. At the same time, around 120 organizations were identified from Coimbatore industrial association (Tamil Nadu) since a comparative study between two states were done. Based on the information provided by them the master list of organizations was prepared. Before collecting main data from the organizations, it is required to ensure the following aspects with respect to the measuring instrument developed.

1. To test the applicability of the questionnaire
2. To analyze the responsiveness of the measuring instrument.
3. To measure the reliability of the questionnaire
4. To measure the validity of the questionnaire.
5. To plan the main study.

R. Srinivasan and C.P. Lohith, *Strategic Marketing and Innovation for Indian MSMEs*, India Studies in Business and Economics,
DOI 10.1007/978-981-10-3590-6_6

6.2 The Applicability and Responsiveness of the Questionnaire

A pilot survey is actually the imitation and trail of the main survey. The very purpose of doing a pilot study is to find out any flaw if it exists in the measuring instrument. For ensuring the responsiveness and applicability, the following aspects were taken care during the administration of the questionnaire. The questionnaire contains the right questions relevant to the organization, which are phrased in the least ambiguous manner and are free from bias.

The questionnaire has been administered to the right person(s), i.e. the senior managers of the organizations who are conversant with the strategic marketing practices of the organization and the innovation performance. The questionnaire is very much structured in nature with a proper sequence having detailed instructions for responding.

It is required to administer the questionnaire to a sample of organizations as part of the Pilot study. For the pilot study, the organizations were visited and the concerned Senior Managers were contacted in person. As mentioned in the previous chapter the questionnaire developed consists of two parts:

(1) The basic information regarding the organization
(2) The data on detailed information on Strategic Marketing (SM) and innovation performance collected using the Likert Scale. Each construct of SM and innovation are having a number of items ranging from 10 to 12.

The details of research were explained to the Senior Managers of the organizations and they were asked to fill in the questionnaire developed for the research study. Though it was difficult and time consuming, many of them were cooperative and were kind enough to spend time for answering the questionnaire. Initially the feedback obtained from around 10–15 randomly selected organizations from both Karnataka and Tamil Nadu was analyzed for the pilot study.

6.3 Data Preparation

Raw data from the research project cannot be directly used for analysis. Raw data is in the form of source documents—completed questionnaires, interview schedules, observation sheets or records of different types. Hence from the raw data an initial database is prepared which is in the form of a data matrix in which the rows are the records of a particular organization under study and columns corresponds to the specific variables. Here in this case a total of four variables of SM are having a total of 48 items and five variables of innovation having a total of 50 items. A portion of the sample of initial database is depicted Table 6.1.

Table 6.1 Initial database (part)

	X_{1-1}	X_{1-2}	X_{1-3}	X_{1-4}	X_{5-8}	X_{5-9}	X_{5-10}
O_1	4	3	5	5	4	3	4
O_2	5	4	5	4	2	2	3
O_3	4	4	5	5	4	3	4
O_4	4	3	4	4	4	4	3
O_n							

The steps involved in the preparation of this initial database are

1. Editing data—verification for missing data, ambiguous data, accuracy, quality etc. in the questionnaire.
2. Coding data—conversion of raw data into symbols and numerals. Here in this research the organizations are identified as O_1, O_2, O_3 ...etc. Variables are identified as X_1, X_2, ...X_4 and Y_1, Y_2,.... Y_5, and the items under each variables as X_{1-1}, X_{1-2}.... etc. and Y_{2-1}, Y_{2-2} etc.
3. Transcription of data—here the data i.e., the responses on the questionnaires is physically transferred to the database from the questionnaire by the manual data entry process.

6.4 Validity and Reliability in Measurement

Knowing that errors will creep into measurements in practice, it is necessary to evaluate the accuracy and dependability of the measuring instrument. The criteria for such evaluations are validity, reliability and practicality. Validity refers to the extent to which a test/instrument measures what it actually intend to measure. Reliability has to do with the accuracy and precision of a measurement procedure. Practicality is concerned with a wide range of factors of economy, convenience, and interpretability (Krishnaswamy et al. 2006). For the pilot study, a preliminary analysis of the collected data was carried out for checking the reliability and validity of the questionnaire developed.

6.4.1 Validity—Multitrait Multimethod Matrix

A scale or measuring instrument is said to posses' validity to the extent to which differences in measured values reflect true differences in the characteristics or property being measured (Krishnaswamy et al. 2006). Validity is the extent to which a scale or set of measures accurately represents the concept of interest (Hair et al. 2007). Here we are interested in the internal validity of the measuring instrument.

Internal validity is the extent to which differences found with a measuring tool reflect true differences among those being tested. The widely accepted classification of validity consist of three major forms—content, criterion and construct (Krishnaswamy et al. 2006). Content validity is the extent to which the instrument provides adequate coverage of the topic under study. This is judgmental in nature and requires generally a panel of judges and accurate definitions of the topic. Face validity is the minimum index of content validity. In the current research, we have ensured the content validity in the literature survey and research design stage itself by giving the accurate definitions of topic under study. In addition, we sought opinions from people from the industry and fellow researchers on the instrument developed. Criterion related validity is an external validity, which reflects the success of measures used for some empirical estimating purposes. Construct validity testifies to how well the results obtained from the use of the measure fits the theory around which the test is designed. It is involved with the factors that lies behind the measurement scores obtained; with what factors or characteristics (that is constructs) account for or explains the variance in measurement scores. Also, it may be required to measure or infer the presence of abstract characteristics for which no empirical validation is possible. Summated scales like likert scale generally concern concepts that fall in this category. Even though this validation situation is much more difficult it is necessary to have some assurance that the measurement has an acceptable degree of validity. Construct validity is assessed through convergent validity and discriminant validity. Convergent validity assesses the degree to which two measures of the same concept are correlated and high correlations here indicate that the scale is measuring the intended concept. Discriminant validity is the degree to which two conceptually similar concepts are distinct and low correlations here indicate that the scale is sufficiently different from the other concept.

One of the widely used methods of simultaneously establishing convergent and discriminant validity is the multitrait and multimethod matrix (MTMM). The basic concept of MTMM is that correlation among the scores of the same construct should be the largest correlations in the matrix (Krishnaswamy et al. 2006).

In the current research, the data collected from the pilot study the initial database as per Table 6.1 is analyzed using SPSS (Software package for social sciences). The correlation coefficients of measures of all the four constructs of SM and measures of all the five constructs of innovation were found out. Tables 6.2 and 6.3 give the average correlation between the scores of different constructs for both independent and dependent variables respectively.

The concept of convergent validity is extended further by thinking of a measure that has multiple items, for instance, the 10–12 items scale designed to measure SM and Innovation in our present research. If the items actually do reflect the construct of SM or innovation, then it is expected that the average intercorrelation values are the highest in the matrix. This condition is satisfied in our present work and thereby supports convergent validity.

Discriminant validity is the principle that measures of theoretically different constructs should not correlate highly with each other. In the current research each of the constructs of SM and Innovation are measured using different items. It is expected that, because these are measures of different constructs, the average cross-construct correlations would be low. These low correlations are evidence for

Table 6.2 Average correlation between scores of SM constructs

Karnataka study				
	X_1	X_2	X_3	X_4
X_1	1	0.29	0.46	0.44
X_2	0.46	1	0.18	−0.07
X_3	0.46	0.18	1	0.07
X_4	0.04	−0.07	0.07	1
Tamil Nadu study				
	X_1	X_2	X_3	X_4
X_1	1	0.26	0.43	0.40
X_2	0.43	1	0.16	−0.05
X_3	0.44	0.16	1	0.04
X_4	0.02	−0.05	0.04	1

Table 6.3 Average correlation between scores of innovation constructs

Karnataka study					
	Y_1	Y_2	Y_3	Y_4	Y_5
Y_1	1	0.22	0.217	0.141	0.257
Y_2	0.22	1	0.160	0.32	−0.012
Y_3	0.217	0.160	1	0.231	−0.155
Y_4	0.141	0.327	0.231	1	0.029
Y_5	0.257	−0.012	−0.155	0.029	1
Tamil Nadu study					
	Y_1	Y_2	Y_3	Y_4	Y_5
Y_1	1	0.18	0.213	0.130	0.234
Y_2	0.18	1	0.140	0.42	−0.016
Y_3	0.213	0.140	1	0.121	0.133
Y_4	0.130	0.42	0.121	1	0.012
Y_5	0.234	−0.016	0.133	0.012	1

discriminant validity. Finally, when all these are put together, both convergent and discriminant validity could be addressed simultaneously. Here, the four constructs of SM are measured with different items. In Tables 6.2 and 6.3, the highlighted correlations are within-construct ones. They are a reflection of convergent validity and are the maximum compared to others. The non-highlighted correlations are cross-construct, reflect discriminant validity, and are uniformly lower than the convergent coefficients. This establishes convergent and discriminant validity. Hence, it can be seen that the validity of the measuring instrument is ensured since the average inter correlation between the scores of the same construct is the largest correlation in the matrix.

6.4.2 Reliability—Cronbach Alpha

The reliability of a measure indicates the stability and consistency with which the instrument measures the concept and helps to assess the goodness of a measure. A measure is reliable to the degree that it supplies consistent results. Reliability is partial contributor to validity. A measuring instrument which is reliable may not be a valid one, but a valid instrument should be reliable (Krishnaswamy et al. 2006).

Reliability is an assessment of the degree of consistency between multiple measurements of a variable. There are two forms of reliability one is the test-retest and the other one is the more commonly used one is the internal consistency (Hair et al. 2007). Here in the current research we have adopted the second form i.e. the internal consistency, which applies to the consistency among the variables in a summated scale.

Inter item consistency reliability is a test of the consistency of the respondent's responses to all the items in a measure. To the degree that the items are independent measures of the same concept, they will be correlated with one another. The most popular test of inter item consistency reliability is Cronbach's alpha which is used for multipoint scaled items.

Cronbach alpha is a reliability coefficient that assesses the consistency of the entire scale. The generally agreed upon lower limit for Cronbach alpha is 0.70 although it may decrease to 0.60 in exploratory research (Hair et al. 2007).

The data collected from the pilot study the initial database as per Table 6.1 is analyzed using SPSS (Statistical Package for the Social Sciences) for validity and reliability analysis. Tables 6.4 and 6.5 give the Cronbach alpha of different constructs for both independent and dependent variables respectively.

From the above tables it can be seen that the measurement scale is highly reliable indicating even the lowest value of Cronbach alpha being 0.620. For ensuring the validity further data reduction has been carried out by confirmatory factor analysis.

Table 6.4 Cronbach alpha for independent variables of SM

Karnataka study			
Strategic marketing constructs	Independent variables	No. of items	Cronbach alpha
Environmental landscaping	X_1	12	0.885
Marketing mix	X_2	12	0.755
Brand positioning	X_3	12	0.965
Entrepreneurial management	X_4	12	0.790
Tamil Nadu study			
Strategic marketing constructs	Independent variables	No. of items	Cronbach alpha
Environmental landscaping	X_1	12	0.816
Marketing mix	X_2	12	0.823
Brand positioning	X_3	12	0.819
Entrepreneurial management	X_4	12	0.845

Table 6.5 Cronbach alpha for dependent variables of innovation

Karnataka study			
Innovation performance constructs	Dependent variables	No. of items	Cronbach alpha
Technological innovation	Y_1	10	0.837
Product innovation	Y_2	10	0.798
Process innovation	Y_3	10	0.815
System innovation	Y_4	10	0.620
Innovation management	Y_5	10	0.706
Tamil Nadu study			
Innovation performance constructs	Dependent variables	No. of items	Cronbach alpha
Technological innovation	Y_1	10	0.901
Product innovation	Y_2	10	0.854
Process innovation	Y_3	10	0.797
System innovation	Y_4	10	0.701
Innovation management	Y_5	10	0.802

Chapter 7 gives details on the confirmatory factor analysis carried out on the complete data collected during main study.

6.5 Review Questions

1. Explain the need of doing a pilot study in the quantitative research.
2. Explain the concept of validity and how do check the validity of a structured questionnaire.
3. Explain the concept of reliability and how do check the reliability of a structured questionnaire.
4. What is data preparation? Explain the steps involved in the preparation of initial data base.

Referenccs

Krishnaswamy KN et al. (2006) Management research methodology, 1st edn. Pearson Education

Hair JF Jr, Black WC, Babin BJ, Anderson RE, Tatham RL (2007) Multivariate data analysis, Ch. 1, 2 & 4, 6th edn. Pearson Prentice Hall

Chapter 7
Main Study—Data Reduction and Confirmatory Factor Analysis

Abstract The main research study consists of obtaining feedback through the questionnaire developed from all the organizations identified for data collection. In this context, a sample size of 270 organizations was considered for the main study. Out of 270 samples, 150 are from Bangalore region (Karnataka) and remaining 120 from Coimbatore region (Tamil Nadu) were taken for the current study. The initial database prepared is expanded by transcribing all the data obtained from the 91 organizations each from Karnataka and Tamil Nadu respectively through the questionnaire and the final database is prepared. The next stage in data analysis is the data reduction, which is the transformation of information. It is derived empirically or experimentally into corrected, ordered and simplified form which is achieved by confirmatory factor analysis.

Key takeaways

1. Transcribing the data during reduction of data.
2. Confirmatory factor analysis.
3. Concept of summated scale.

Keywords Questionnaire · Non-probability sampling · Confirmatory factor analysis · Hypothesis test · Reflective measurement theory · Summated scale

7.1 Data Collection For Main Study

The main research study consists of obtaining feedback through the questionnaire developed from all the organizations identified for data collection. Response rate is an important factor for getting sufficient data. In our present study the sampling procedure adopted was non-probability sampling, which is based on judgment sampling and purposive sampling. In this context, a sample size of 270 organizations was considered for the main study. Out of 270 samples, 150 are from Bangalore region (Karnataka) and remaining 120 from Coimbatore region (Tamil Nadu) were taken for the current study. To increase the response rates the following additional actions were also initiated by us:

R. Srinivasan and C.P. Lohith, *Strategic Marketing and Innovation for Indian MSMEs*, India Studies in Business and Economics,
DOI 10.1007/978-981-10-3590-6_7

Table 7.1 Response rate

Karnataka study				
	Micro	Small scale	Medium scale	Total
Number of organizations contacted	15	75	70	150
Number of organizations responded	04	38	49	91
Response rate percentage (%)	26.66	50.66	70.00	60.66
Tamil Nadu study				
	Micro	Small scale	Medium scale	Total
Number of organizations Contacted	10	45	65	120
Number of organizations responded	5	32	54	91
Response rate percentage (%)	50.00	71.11	83.07	75.83

1. The survey was administered to the intended respondents and it was designed user friendly.
2. The measuring instrument was designed with relevant questions with a nice layout.
3. Prenotifications were made to ensure higher response rate.
4. Timely follow-ups and prompt acknowledgements were made.

All these precautions resulted in an overall good response rate of 60.6% the details of which are represented in Table 7.1.

For Multiple Regression this sample of observations very well meets the guideline for the minimum ratio of observations to independent variables (5:1) (Hair et al. 2007). With 91 organizations, this ratio becomes around 22:1 with 4 independent variables. For reasons of confidentiality, the names of organizations and respondents are not revealed. However, the characteristics of the organizations from where data is collected are as given below:

1. Organizations and contact details are identified with the help of MSME Development Institute of Bangalore and Peenya Industries Association, Bangalore of Karnataka and Coimbatore Industrial Association of Tamil Nadu.
2. Organizations consist of micro, small and medium manufacturing organizations of Indian origin.
3. Each organization considered as a sampling unit, is a Strategic Business Unit irrespective of they are micro or small or medium scale.

The initial database prepared is expanded by transcribing all the data obtained from the 91 organizations each from Karnataka and Tamil Nadu respectively through the questionnaire and the final database is prepared. A portion of the final database format is depicted in Table 7.2. The next stage in data analysis is the data reduction, which is the transformation of information. It is derived empirically or experimentally into corrected, ordered and simplified form. This is achieved by confirmatory factor analysis.

Table 7.2 Final database

	X_{1-1}	X_{1-2}	X_{1-3}	x_{1-4}	Y_{5-08}	Y_{5-09}	Y_{5-10}
O_1	4	3	5	5	4	3	4
O_2	5	4	5	4	2	2	3
O_3	4	4	5	5	4	3	4
O_4	4	3	4	4	4	4	3
O_5	5	4	5	4	2	2	3
O_{91}							

7.2 Confirmatory Factor Analysis

A factor analysis provides two distinct, but interrelated, outcomes: data summarization and data reduction. Data reduction derives an empirical value (factor score) for each variable (factor) and then substituting this value for the original values. Factor analysis achieves data reduction by identifying representative variables from a much larger set of variables for use in subsequent multivariate analysis. It creates an entirely new set of variables much smaller in number, to partially or completely replace the original set of variables (Hair et al. 2007). Regarding sample size for factor analysis generally, the minimum is to have at least five times as many observations as the number of variables to be analyzed, and the more acceptable sample size would have 10:1 ratio. In general, for sample size—the sample must have more observations than Variables and the minimum absolute sample size should be 50 observations (Hair et al. 2007). This has been ensured in the current research.

Confirmatory factor analysis (CFA) is a factor analysis procedure to test the hypothesis regarding how well the data fits a specified pattern of factor loadings. This may include the number and nature of factors corresponding to prior theoretical notions (Krishnaswamy et al. 2006).

CFA seeks to determine if the number of factors and the loadings of measured (indicator) variables on them conform to what is expected based on pre-established theory. Indicator variables are selected based on prior theory and factor analysis is used to see if they load as predicted on the expected number of factors. The preliminary assumption is that each factor (the number and labels of which may be specified à priori) is associated with a specified subset of indicator variables. A minimum requirement of confirmatory factor analysis is to hypothesize beforehand the number of factors in the model. It is determined; for instance, if measures created to represent a latent variable really belong together.

The questionnaire developed for the current research uses the reflective measurement theory. A reflective measurement theory is based on the idea that latent construct cause the measured variables and an error results in an inability to fully explain these measures. With reflective models any item that is not expected to correlate highly with the other indicators of a factor are to be deleted.

7.3 Factor Loadings

Factor loadings are the correlation of each variable and the factor. In the current research, this refers to the correlation of each item (sub variable) and the variable. The factor loadings, also called component loadings in principal component analysis are the correlation coefficients between the sub variables (items) and factors (variables). These factor loadings could be interpreted for establishing the validity. An optimal structure exists when all variables have high loadings only on a single factor. Squared factor loadings indicate what percentage of the variance in an original variable is explained by a factor.

According to Hair et al. (2007):

1. Factor loadings in the range ±0.30 to ±0.40 are considered to meet the minimal level for interpretation of structure.
2. Loadings ±0.5 or greater are considered practically significant and are generally considered necessary.
3. Loadings exceeding ±0.7 are considered indicative of well defined structure and are the goal of any factor analysis.

In confirmatory factor analysis, the number of factors that exist within a set of variables as well as which factor will each load highly is specified before results can be computed. In CFA, statistics tell how well the specification of the factors matches reality (the actual data). Thus, CFA is a tool that enables to either confirm or reject preconceived theory. In the current research, we have specified the number factors i.e. the constructs (variables) of Strategic marketing and Innovation and the corresponding sub variables i.e. the items that describe these constructs.

The approach is a confirmatory factor analysis and it is not a factor analysis for reallocation of items/dimensions among constructs. (One is a bottom up approach and the other one is a top down approach). The purpose was to select items, which are highly representative in nature. In this process, the factors (constructs) are predefined and the factor loadings will decide whether an item can be considered for a factor. Due to built in redundancy, more number of items are available for each construct, and are allocation of items is not attempted.

Confirmatory factor analysis on the data collected from main study the final database as per Table 7.2 is carried out using SPSS for data reduction and factor analysis. Tables 7.3 and 7.4 give the factor loadings (rounded to two decimal places) of all the items of the dependent variables of innovation performance and all the items of the independent variables of Strategic marketing respectively. In the table, the item no. represents the statement number (sub variable) in the questionnaire, corresponding to the variables Y_1 to Y_5 and X_1 to X_4, which represent the variables (constructs) of innovation performance and strategic marketing respectively.

Factor loadings in the range of

0.3–0.4: Meet the minimum level for interpretation of the structure.

≥ 0.5: practically significant and are generally considered necessary.

>0.7: considered indicative of well defined structure and are the goal of any factor analysis.

Table 7.3 CFA—factor loadings of variables of innovation performance

Karnataka study					
Item no.	Y_1	Y_2	Y_3	Y_4	Y_5
1	0.810	0.682	0.442	0.779	0.770
2	0.498	0.432	0.837	0.635	0.794
3	0.756	0.665	0.858	0.564	0.819
4	0.729	0.722	0.635	0.787	0.477
5	0.563	0.800	0.347	0.600	0.526
6	0.801	0.494	0.367	0.629	0.622
7	0.764	0.901	0.593	0.582	0.439
8	0.627	0.810	0.771	0.795	0.678
9	0.811	0.402	0.890	0.663	0.854
10	0.603	0.594	0.841	0.643	0.840
Tamil Nadu study					
Item no.	Y_1	Y_2	Y_3	Y_4	Y_5
1	0.790	0.615	0.501	0.801	0.690
2	0.501	0.414	0.799	0.613	0.802
3	0.745	0.699	0.849	0.602	0.798
4	0.734	0.741	0.615	0.798	0.532
5	0.598	0.786	0.412	0.599	0.515
6	0.799	0.451	0.354	0.602	0.599
7	0.725	0.899	0.602	0.593	0.425
8	0.627	0.799	0.745	0.756	0.608
9	0.789	0.525	0.902	0.701	0.869
10	0.599	0.587	0.851	0.663	0.896

The confirmatory factor analysis almost also confirms the earlier results of validity found out by multitrait multi method matrix. If a cut of value of 0.4 is taken as lower level value then, out of the 98 items only for 3 items the loading is less than 0.4. If a cut of value of 0.7 is taken as lower level value then, out of 98 items only 52 items are loading less than 0.7 and 46 items are retained. If a cut off value of 0.5 is taken as lower level value then, out of 98 items only 17 items are loading less than 0.5 and 81 items are retained. In the current research, we have taken a cut off value of 0.5 for the loadings. Tables 7.3 and 7.4 give the factor loadings rounded to two decimal places, and only items for which the factor loading values are actually greater than or equal to 0.5 are considered for further analysis. The modified details of items used for further analysis is given Table 7.5.

With respect to Karnataka study, the 17 items that are having a factor loading less than 0.5, are excluded, and are not included for further analysis. Out of 98 items, 81 items loading on 9 variables is a clear indication of the variables and items supporting the theory. With respect to Tamil Nadu study, there were totally 10 items that are having factor loadings less than 0.5. Hence 10 items are excluded

Table 7.4 CFA—factor loadings of variables of strategic marketing performance

Karnataka study				
Item no.	X_1	X_2	X_3	X_4
1	0.544	0.370	0.532	0.602
2	0.445	0.614	0.737	0.381
3	0.476	0.444	0.492	0.774
4	0.533	0.382	0.734	0.561
5	0.770	0.538	0.799	0.648
6	0.687	0.681	0.754	0.760
7	0.656	0.672	0.656	0.463
8	0.810	0.700	0.758	0.617
9	0.662	0.750	0.862	0.770
10	0.627	0.822	0.788	0.708
11	0.820	0.903	0.783	0.785
12	0.633	0.658	0.742	0.689
Tamil Nadu study				
Item no.	X_1	X_2	X_3	X_4
1	0.512	0.336	0.568	0.599
2	0.502	0.715	0.799	0.413
3	0.526	0.567	0.499	0.713
4	0.567	0.399	0.699	0.517
5	0.690	0.568	0.803	0.659
6	0.699	0.705	0.799	0.800
7	0.691	0.703	0.612	0.588
8	0.797	0.698	0.881	0.675
9	0.702	0.801	0.835	0.745
10	0.601	0.799	0.756	0.699
11	0.799	0.925	0.805	0.806
12	0.678	0.631	0.705	0.645

from further analysis, out of 98 items, 88 items are considered. Even if the factor loadings are to be interpreted in the light of theory and not by arbitrary cut-off levels, few items are deleted mainly to improve the validity of the exercise. Even though some dimensions under each construct, which apparently seems to be more representative of the construct got knocked out, due to sufficient redundancy these may not be having a major implication in the data analysis. The factor loading itself is an indicator, which conveys about the knocked out variables do not actually measure what is intended to be measured due to absence of validity.

Moreover, here in the current research a reflective measurement theory is used which is based on the idea that 'latent constructs' cause the measured variable (Hair et al. 2007). If all the indicator items share a common conceptual basis meaning they all indicate the same thing, then the measurement model is best considered reflective. Also, latent constructs should be indicated by at least three measured variables preferably four or more and here the minimum number of items is ten.

When all items represent the same concept, dropping an item does not materially change a construct's meaning (Hair et al. 2007). Hence, the reliability and robustness of further analysis and results is not going to be affected much.

Variables communality is the estimate of its shared or common variance among the variables as represented by the derived factors. Once all the significant loadings have been identified, it is required to look for any variables, which are not adequately accounted for by the factor solution. Here the communality of each variable is examined to assess whether the variables meet acceptable levels of explanation. Using this guideline, all variables with communalities less than 0.5 are identified as not having sufficient explanation. This has been examined and after identification of significant loadings all the variables is having communality values greater than 0.5 and are sufficiently explained.

When specifying the number of indicators (items) per variable (construct) it is recommended to use more than four indicators whenever possible (Hair et al. 2007). We have ensured this also in the current research. From Table 7.5 it can be observed that the number of items per construct is not less than ten.

Table 7.5 Modified number of items in each variable

Karnataka study							
Strategic marketing				Innovation performance			
Independent variables (IV)				Dependent variables (DV)			
IV	Number of items			DV	Number of items		
	Original	Deleted	Retained		Original	Deleted	Retained
X_1	12	2	10	Y_1	10	1	09
X_2	12	3	09	Y_2	10	3	07
X_3	12	1	11	Y_3	10	3	07
X_4	12	2	10	Y_4	10	0	10
-	-	-	-	Y_5	10	2	08
Total	48	08	40	Total	50	9	41
Tamil Nadu study							
Strategic marketing Independent variables (IV)				Innovation performance Dependent variables (DV)			
IV	Number of items			DV	Number of items		
	Original	Deleted	Retained		Original	Deleted	Retained
X_1	12	1	11	Y_1	10	1	09
X_2	12	1	10	Y_2	10	1	09
X_3	12	1	11	Y_3	10	2	08
X_4	12	1	11	Y_4	10	0	10
-	-	-	-	Y_5	10	1	09
Total	48	08	43	Total	50	9	45

7.4 Creating Summated Scales

All the variables loading highly on a factor are combined, and the total—or more commonly the average score of the variables is used as replacement variable. Here such a summated scale has two benefits.

1. It provides a means of overcoming the measurement error inherent in all measured variables.
2. Second benefit of summated scale is its ability to represent the multiple aspects of a concept in a single measure.

Taking the average of the items in the scale provides complete control over the calculation and facilitates ease of use in subsequent analysis (Hair et al. 2007).

Though summated scales include only the variable that load highly on the factor and excludes those having little or marginal impact, it has the following advantages:

1. Compromises between the surrogate variable and the factor score options.
2. Reduces measurement error.
3. Represents the multiple facets of a concept.
4. Easily replicable across studies.

Summated scale requires extensive analysis of reliability and validity and it has been discussed already in Chap. 6. If a summated scale is well-constructed, valid, and reliable instrument, then it is the best alternative, which renders generalisablity and transferability (Hair et al. 2007). This summated scale has been constructed and the details of the data are presented in Chap. 8.

7.5 Review Questions

1. How do you increase the response rate during the main data collection?
2. Explain the concept of Confirmatory factor analysis.
3. What is summated scale? How do you create it?
4. Elaborate on the advantages of summated scale.

References

Hair JF Jr, Black WC, Babin BJ, Anderson RE, Tatham RL (2007) Multivariate data analysis, Ch. 1, 2 & 4, 6th edn. Pearson Prentice Hall

Krishnaswamy KN et al (2006) Management Research Methodology, 1st edn. Pearson Education

Chapter 8
Main Study—Data Preparation and Preliminary Data Analysis

Abstract The previous chapter was concluded by addressing about the creation of summated scale from the main study data collected by confirmatory factor analysis. This chapter discusses about the actual creation of such a summated data from the main study data and a preliminary analysis of that data. The transcription and summation of data is carried out on a data summary spreadsheet prepared in Microsoft excel. The average score of each Strategic Marketing and innovation constructs for all the organizations was found out and a summarized score table was tabulated. The information is also depicted in the form of graphical representations.

Key takeaways:

1. Creating summated data from the main study data.
2. Preliminary data analysis.
3. Developing constructs of strategic marketing and innovation.

Keywords Data transcription · Data summation · Constructs multi variate analysis · Linear trends

8.1 Creation of Summated Data and Transcription

The previous chapter was concluded by addressing about the creation of summated scale from the main study data collected. This chapter discusses about the actual creation of such a summated data from the main study data and a preliminary analysis of that data.

The transcription and summation of data is carried out on a data summary spreadsheet prepared in Microsoft excel (Table 8.1). Due to constraints of space, Table 8.1 depicts only a few organizations.

The data summary spreadsheet has three parts, which is in line with the questionnaire used for primary data collection, and they are:

R. Srinivasan and C.P. Lohith, *Strategic Marketing and Innovation for Indian MSMEs*, India Studies in Business and Economics,
DOI 10.1007/978-981-10-3590-6_8

Table 8.1 Main study data summary of studies done at Karnataka and Tamil Nadu (partly depicted)

Karnataka and Tamil Nadu							
Organisations		V	O_1	O_2	O_3	O_{91}	Total
Constructs of SM							
1	Environmental landscaping	X_1	5.00 4.99	4.40 4.98	3.80 3.90	4.40 4.50	4.27 4.33
2	Marketing mix	X_2	4.10 4.36	4.70 4.51	4.40 3.98	3.88 4.01	4.04 4.12
3	Brand positioning	X_3	4.36 4.27	4.72 4.76	4.27 4.32	4.36 4.21	4.07 4.19
4	Entrepreneurial management	X_4	4.80 4.33	4.70 4.56	4.40 4.33	4.70 4.57	4.32 4.23
Average SM performance			4.56 4.67	4.63 4.36	4.21 4.27	4.33 4.11	4.21 4.55
Constructs of Innovation							
1	Technological innovation	Y_1	5.00 4.78	4.33 4.55	4.22 4.78	4.44 4.52	4.11 4.55
2	Product innovation	Y_2	5.00 4.98	3.57 3.66	3.85 3.78	4.42 4.32	3.90 3.97
3	Process innovation	Y_3	4.85 4.78	4.28 4.33	4.14 4.23	4.57 4.59	4.17 4.23
4	System innovation	Y_4	5.00 4.89	4.55 4.42	4.11 4.23	4.66 4.45	4.41 4.23
5	Innovation management	Y_5	5.00 4.56	4.50 4.36	4.00 3.99	4.77 4.33	4.35 4.56
Average innovation performance			4.97 4.78	4.24 4.33	4.06 4.14	4.57 4.67	4.18 4.38
Organisation features							
1	Size of organization (M/S/M)		M	S	M		91
2	Type of manufacturing industry		04 05	38 32	49 54		91 91

1. Constructs of SM (Strategic Marketing), consisting the summated data of the independent variables of SM.
2. Constructs of innovation, consisting the summated data of the dependent variables of innovation performance.
3. Organization features consisting of size of organization, industry type.

8.2 Constructs of SM and Innovation

The summated score for each construct of SM and innovation are calculated by the methodology explained in Chap. 6 i.e.

Score for the construct = (Sum of the response values for the statements)/(Number of statements)

For example, consider the Marketing Mix construct (X_2) of SM wherein 12 items are there. For organization O_1 the score is given by:

Score of $X_2 = (X_{2\text{-}2} + X_{2\text{-}5} + X_{2\text{-}6} + X_{2\text{-}7} + X_{2\text{-}8} + X_{2\text{-}9} + X_{2\text{-}10} + X_{2\text{-}11} + X_{2\text{-}12})/9$

Here it may be specifically pointed out that that summation of 9 items has been carried out. It is to be noted that 3 items from the original data i.e. $X_{2\text{-}1}$, $X_{2\text{-}3}$ *and* $X_{2\text{-}4}$, has been excluded. This is due to their low factor loading values of less than 0.5, which was identified during the confirmatory factor analysis stage.

Similarly taking another example, consider the Process innovation construct (Y_3) of Innovation performance wherein 6 items are there. For organization O_1 the score is given by:

Score of $Y_3 = (Y_{3\text{-}2} + Y_{3\text{-}3} + Y_{3\text{-}4} + Y_{3\text{-}7} + Y_{3\text{-}8} + Y_{3\text{-}9} + Y_{3\text{-}10})/7$

Here also it may be specifically pointed out that summation of 7 items has been carried out. It is to be noted that three item from the original data i.e.

$Y_{3\text{-}1}$, $Y_{3\text{-}5}$ & $Y_{3\text{-}6}$ has been excluded. This is due to its low factor loading values of less than 0.5, which was again identified during the confirmatory factor analysis stage. In a similar way, the scores of all the four constructs of SM and five constructs of Innovation performance are calculated for every organization using the main study data after the confirmatory factor analysis. The data are then transcribed to the data summary spreadsheet (Table 8.1) for further statistical analysis.

8.3 Preliminary Data Analysis

It was indicated in Chap. 7 that, 91 organizations situated in Karnataka responded for the survey. The same survey sample was taken from the Tamil Nadu counterpart since it is a comparative study done between the two states. Preliminary analyses of the data collected from the 91 organizations are done as follows:

8.4 Basic Information Summary on Organization Features

The breakup of the organizations covered for the study is given in Fig. 8.1 in the form of a pie chart. Total number of organizations covered indicates that medium-scale organizations are more in number compared to micro and small scale organizations. The research study does not really distinguish between micro medium and small scale organizations and they are considered together in context with

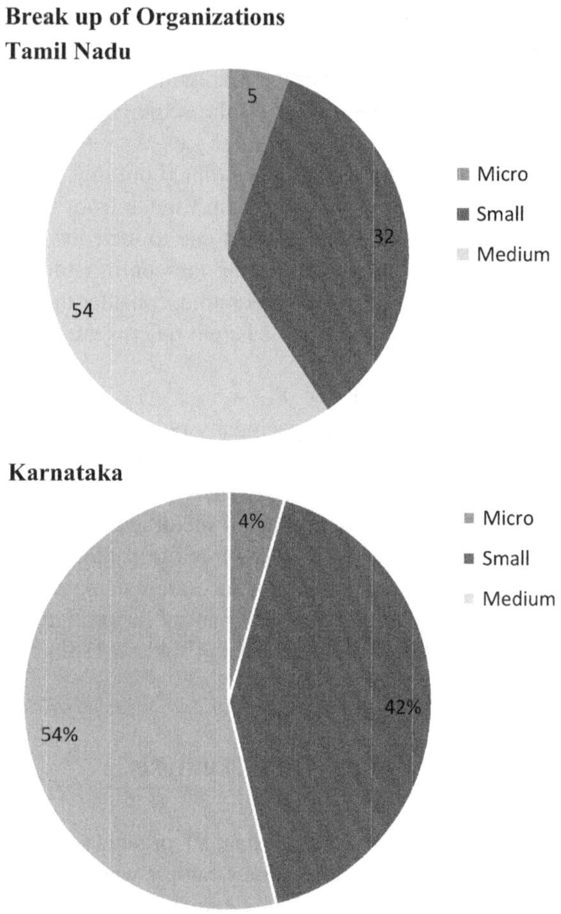

Fig. 8.1 Break ups of organization (colour online)

our research objectives. From the research objective point of view, each organization irrespective of they are micro or small or medium scale are considered as individual strategic business units, which have adopted a set of SM (Strategic Marketing) practices.

The industry wise breakup of organizations is given in Fig. 8.2 in the form of a pie chart. From this chart, it can be seen that almost all the important manufacturing industry sectors got representation in the research study. Moreover, it can also be seen that almost all these sectors are evenly represented. This matter is important from the generalization of findings point of view.

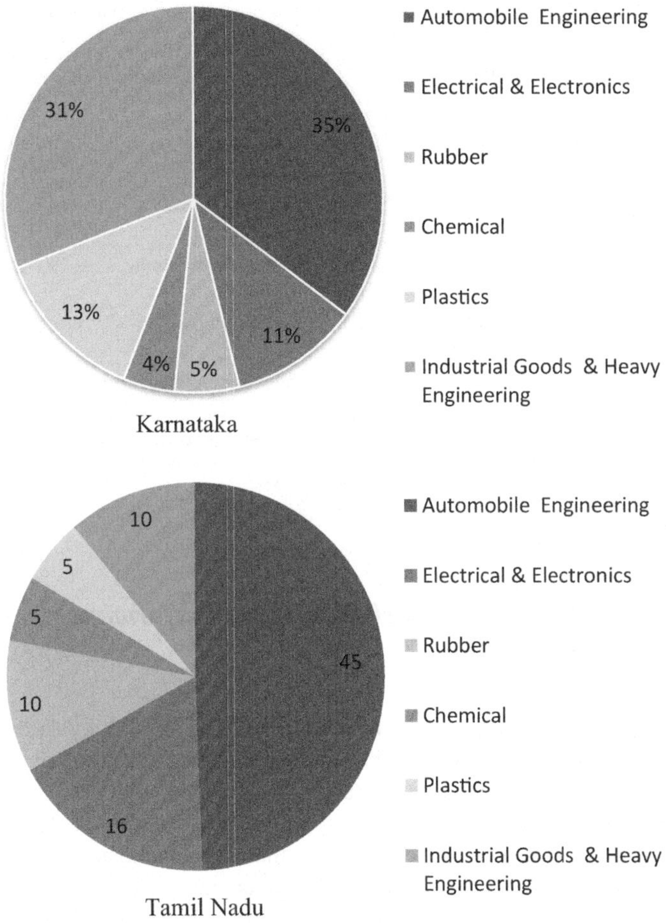

Fig. 8.2 Manufacturing organizations—industry breakup (colour online)

8.5 Strategic Marketing and Innovation Performance Summary

From the data on detailed information on SM and Innovation collected, the main study data summary (Table 8.1), an attempt is made to summarize the overall SM and innovation performance of organizations. In the context the average score of each SM and innovation constructs for all the organizations was found out. This is summarized in Table 8.2. The information is also depicted in the form of column chart in Figs. 8.3 and 8.4.

Table 8.2 Overall SM and innovation performance of organization of both Karnataka and Tamil Nadu

Independent variables of SM			Dependent variables of innovation		
Construct	Variable	Score	Construct	Variable	Score
Environmental landscaping	X_1	4.27[a] 4.33[b]	Technological innovation	Y_1	4.11 4.01
Marketing mix	X_2	4.04 4.21	Product innovation	Y_2	3.90 3.60
Brand positioning	X_3	4.07 4.26	Process innovation	Y_3	4.17 4.23
Entrepreneurial management	X_4	4.32 4.56	System innovation	Y_4	4.41 4.78
			Innovation management	Y_5	4.33 4.41
Overall SM		4.21 4.34	Overall innovation		4.18 4.21

[a]Karnataka
[b]Tamil Nadu

8.5.1 Overall Strategic Marketing (SM) Performance of Organizations

Organizations were evaluated for the four constructs of SM by finding out the average score for each of the four constructs for all organizations put together. It was observed that the maximum score is obtained for the Entrepreneurial Management (4.32) and the minimum score is obtained for the Marketing Mix construct (4.04). This gives an indication that organizations adopting SM are extremely good as far as Entrepreneurial Management aspect is concerned and are lagging as far as Marketing Mix aspect is concerned. Figure 8.3 depicts the overall SM performance of organizations.

The overall SM performance score for all the organizations and all the constructs put together is 4.21, which is indicated by the horizontal line that crosses all the columns in the column chart.

8.5.2 Overall Innovation Performance of Organizations

Organizations were evaluated for the five constructs of innovation by finding out the average score for each of the five constructs for all organizations put together. It was observed that the maximum score is obtained for the system innovation construct (4.41) and minimum score is obtained for the Product Innovation construct (3.90). This gives an indication that organizations adopting Strategic Marketing are extremely doing well as far as System Innovation is concerned and are lagging as

Fig. 8.3 Overall SM performance of organizations (colour online)

far as Product Innovation is concerned. Figure 8.3 depicts the overall innovation performance of organizations.

The overall innovation performance score for all the organizations and all the constructs put together is 4.18, which is indicated by the horizontal line that crosses all the columns in the column chart. This is less than the overall SM performance score of 4.21, which gives an approximate indication that innovation performance, is generally lagging behind SM performance within organizations.

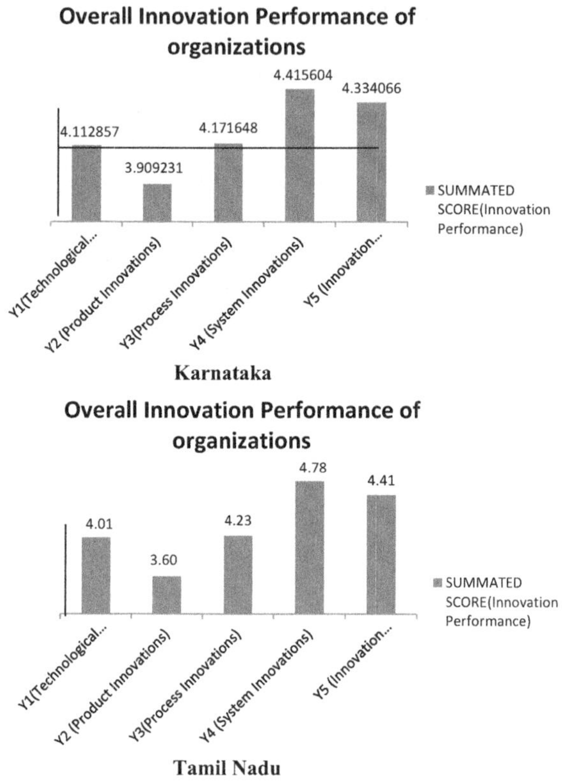

Fig. 8.4 Overall innovation performances of organizations (colour online)

8.6 Trend of Strategic Marketing and Innovation Performance

In order to make an approximate investigation on the relationship of SM to innovation performance it is required to analyze the trend of SM and innovation performance across organizations. For this, the data on SM and innovation performance was arranged in the order of the score of overall SM performance for every organization. The data table illustrating the serial number of organization, SM score and innovation performance score is given in Annexure-I. This data on SM and innovation performance were plotted and a comparison of SM and innovation performance was carried out. This is depicted in Fig. 8.5 trend of SM and innovation performance and Fig. 8.6 linear trend of SM and Innovation performance.

Though the trend chart (Fig. 8.5) shows fluctuations in innovation performance, as the SM performance increases, it can be observed that the innovation performance is also increasing in general. The general innovation performance is low as compared to SM performance except for some of the organizations where innovation performance exceeds SM performance.

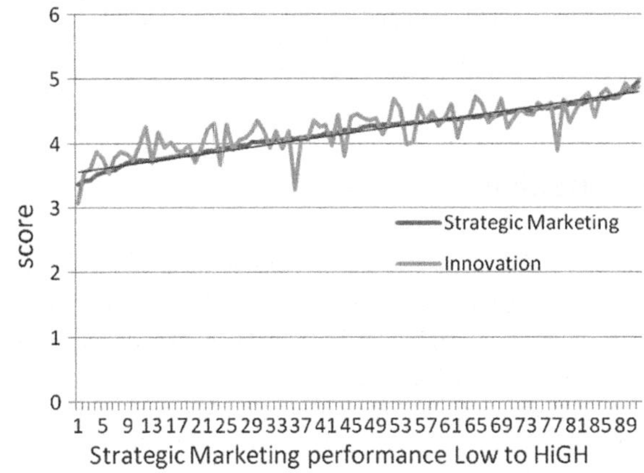

Fig. 8.5 Trends of SM and innovation performance (colour online)

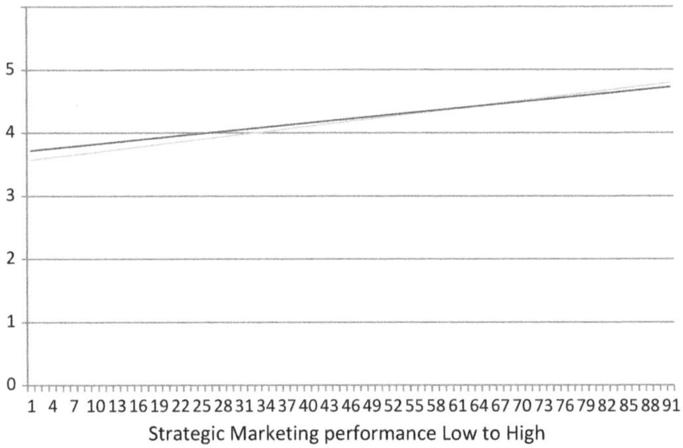

Fig. 8.6 Linear trends of SM and innovation performance

In order to make a better comparison the linear trend lines were plotted for both SM and innovation performance across organizations which is depicted in the linear trend chart (Fig. 8.5). This chart shows a fantastic linear trend with a positive slope. This chart gives indications that SM and innovation performance are almost moving together. As the SM performance increases, innovation performance is also increasing. This is one of the very important findings of this research. This is established in the subsequent chapters wherein the R^2 values obtained for multiple regressions for the various models range from a minimum of 0.504 to a maximum of 0.641.

This relationship is being explored in detail by using the multivariate analysis techniques in the next chapter.

8.7 Review Questions

1. Elaborate on the constructs of strategic marketing and innovation performance identified in the current research.
2. What is preliminary data analysis? Elaborate on the different information collected for doing the preliminary data analysis.
3. Explain the trend of strategic marketing and the innovation performance of Indian MSMEs.

Chapter 9
Main Study—Detailed Statistical Analysis by Multiple Regression

Abstract Out of 150 manufacturing firms, 91 firms responded completely, which was used here for the main data analysis. After the preliminary data analysis done, the detailed statistical analysis of the collected data by multiple regression is attempted in this chapter. The first step in the detailed statistical analysis is the verification of the assumptions underlying multiple regression analysis. Linearity, constant variance (homoscedasticity) and normality are the three assumptions which will be addressed for all the individual variables. Then it proceeds to the estimation of the regression model and assessing the overall model fit.

The key takeaways for the reader from this chapter are listed below

1. Assumptions in multiple regression analysis.
2. Concept of Linearity, Homoscedasticity and Normality.
3. Concept of outliers and influential's.
4. Concept of Multicolinearity.

Keywords Research design · Multiple regression · Independent variable · Dependent variable · Linearity · Homoscedasticity · Normality · Scatter plot matrix · Box plots · Normal probability plot · Skewness · Kurtosis · Outliers · Influentials

9.1 Research Design and Data

The main research study obtained feedback from 91 organizations out of 150 achieving a good response rate of 60.6%. All the 91 firms responded completely, which was used for the main data analysis. The preliminary data analysis has been carried out as explained in Chap. 8. The detailed statistical analysis of the collected data by multiple regression is attempted in this chapter.

R. Srinivasan and C.P. Lohith, *Strategic Marketing and Innovation for Indian MSMEs*, India Studies in Business and Economics,
DOI 10.1007/978-981-10-3590-6_9

9.2 Assumptions in Multiple Regression Analysis

The first step in the detailed statistical analysis is the verification of the assumptions underlying multiple regression analysis. This analysis ensures that the research is meeting the basic assumptions of multiple regression and it involves two steps.

1. Testing the individual dependent and independent variables
2. Testing the overall relationship after model estimation.

Linearity, constant variance (homoscedasticity) and normality are the three assumptions which will be addressed for all the individual variables.

9.3 Linearity

Linearity is examined by the scatter plots of the variables and identification of non-linear patterns in the data (Hair et al. 2007).The scatter plots of individual variables do not indicate any non-linear relationships between the dependent variables and independent variables justifying the assumption of linearity. All the combinations of scatter plots are condensed and the scatter plot matrix between all the dependent and independent variables obtained using SPSS are given in Fig. 9.1. In addition, examples of scatter plots between some independent and dependent variables obtained using SPSS are given in Figs. 9.2, 9.3, 9.4 and 9.5.

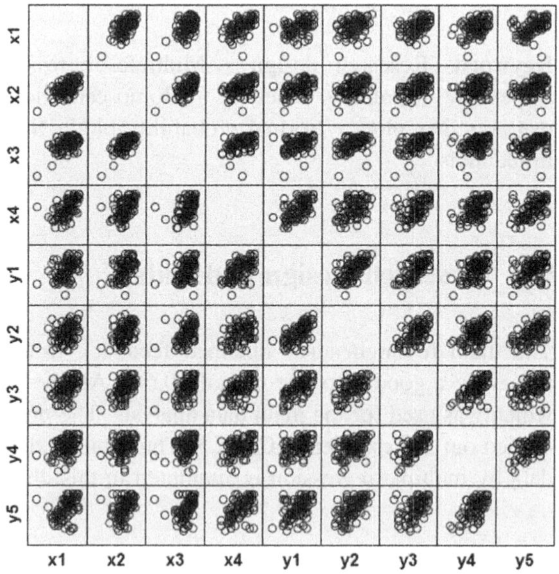

Fig. 9.1 Scatter plot matrix between all dependent and independent variables

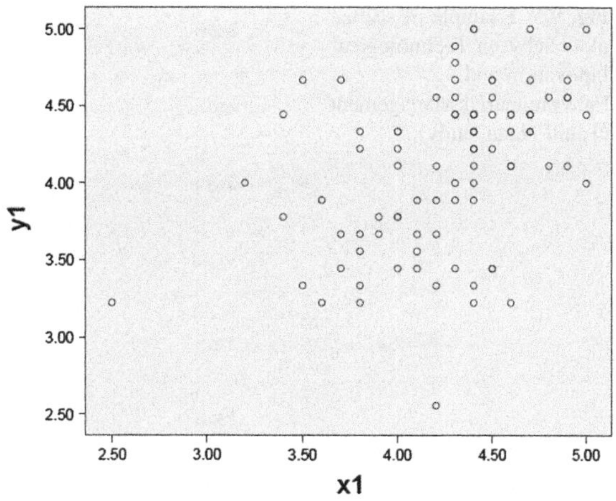

Fig. 9.2 Example of scatter plots between Technological Innovation and Environmental Landscaping (Karnataka study)

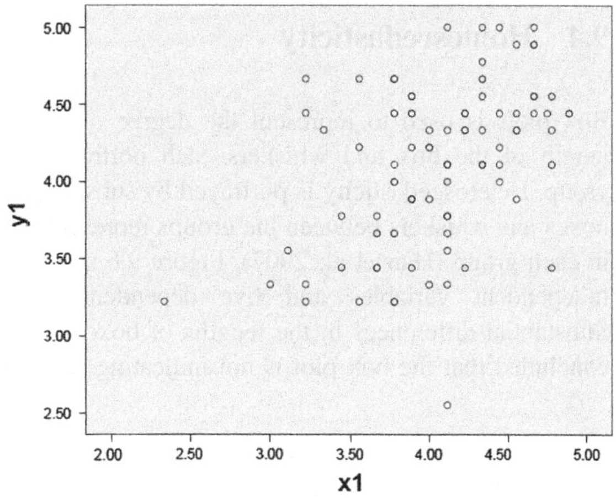

Fig. 9.3 Example of scatter plots between Technological Innovation and Marketing Mix (Karnataka study)

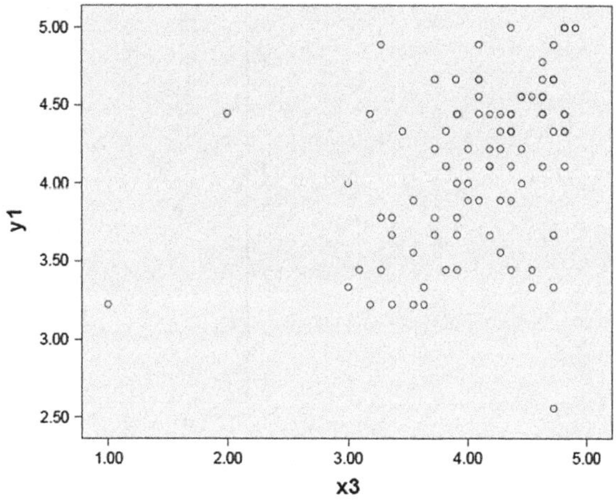

Fig. 9.4 Example of scatter plots between Technological Innovation and Brand Positioning (Tamil Nadu study)

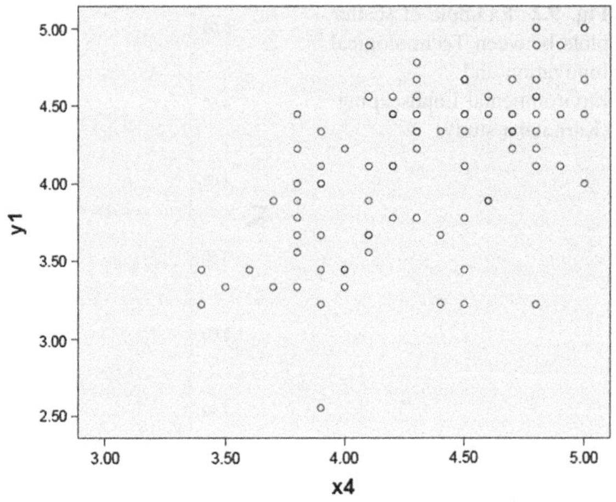

Fig. 9.5 Example of scatter plots between Technological Innovation and Entrepreneurial Management (Tamil Nadu study)

9.4 Homoscedasticity

Box plots is used to represent the degree of variation between the groups. The length of the box and whiskers each portray the variation of data within that group. Heteroscedasticity is portrayed by substantial differences in the length of the boxes and whiskers between the groups representing the dispersion of observations in each group (Hair et al. 2007). Figure 9.6 shows the box plot depicting the four independent variables and five dependent variables obtained using SPSS. Substantial differences in the lengths of boxes could not be noticed and it can be concluded that the box plot is not indicating any heteroscedasticity.

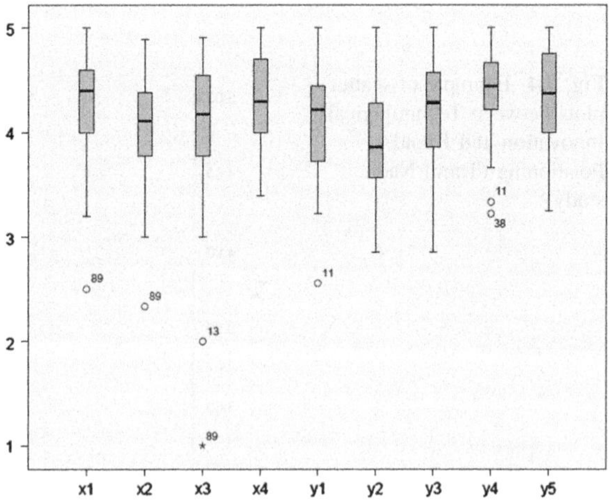

Fig. 9.6 Box plots of variables

Table 9.1 Bartlett's test of homoscedasticity

Groups of variables	K-squared	p-value
Y_1, X_1, X_2, X_3, X_4	9.06859[a] 9.01346[b]	0.3365 0.4321
Y_2, X_1, X_2, X_3, X_4	7.06470 7.13425	0.5297 0.6321
Y_3, X_1, X_2, X_3, X_4	13.04840 11.32445	0.1102 0.2313
Y_4, X_1, X_2, X_3, X_4	6.10760 6.90001	0.6352 0.5671
Y_5X_1, X_2, X_3, X_4	7.90600 8.23123	0.4427 0.3921

[a]Karnataka study
[b]Tamil Nadu study

In addition, the formal tests for testing the equality of variances of all the sets of variables, the Bartlett test for homoscedasticity has been done using R whose results are given in Table 9.1.

The *p*-value of all the original variables are more than 0.05 indicates that the null hypothesis of homoscedasticity cannot be rejected.

9.5 Normality

The next assumption in multivariate analysis is normality. This could be ascertained by referring to the shape of the data distribution for an individual metric variable and its correspondence to the normal distribution (Hair et al. 2007).

A normal probability plot compares the cumulative distribution of actual data values with the cumulative distribution of a normal distribution. If the distribution is normal, the line representing the actual data distribution closely follows the diagonal (Hair et al. 2007). The normal probability plots of independent and dependent variables obtained using SPSS is given in Figs. 9.7, 9.8, 9.9, 9.10, 9.11, 9.12, 9.13, 9.14 and 9.15.

In the normal probability plot, the normal distribution forms a straight diagonal line, and the plotted data values are compared with the diagonal. The normal probability plots though slightly in favour of normality show minor departures from normal distribution for some variables. Formal tests are also performed to ascertain the same. Formal tests provide enough evidence to assume that the quantitative variables have underlying normal distribution. The Shapiro Wilks normality test calculates the level of significance for the differences from a normal distribution and this test was conducted using SPSS on all the variables. The results of the Shapiro Wilks normality tests indicated that the *p* values for some of the variables are less than 0.05 leading to the rejection of null hypotheses of normality in case of some variables. As a remedy for non-normality, though data transformations were tried out for each variable, much improvement was not noticed. Hence, it was decided to

Fig. 9.7 Normal probability plots of independent variables (Karnataka study)

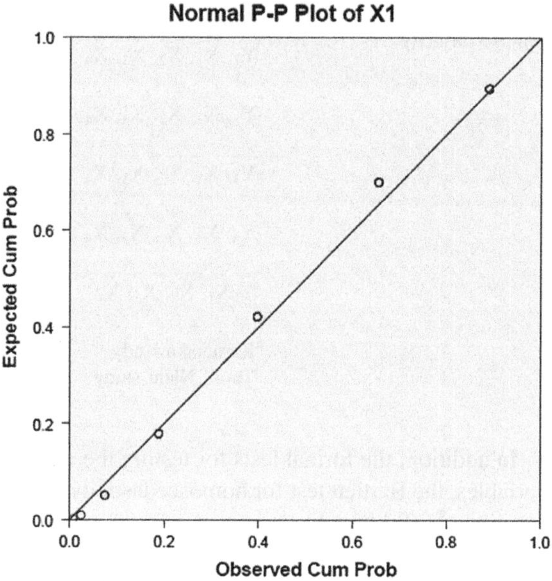

Fig. 9.8 Normal probability plots of independent variables (Karnataka study)

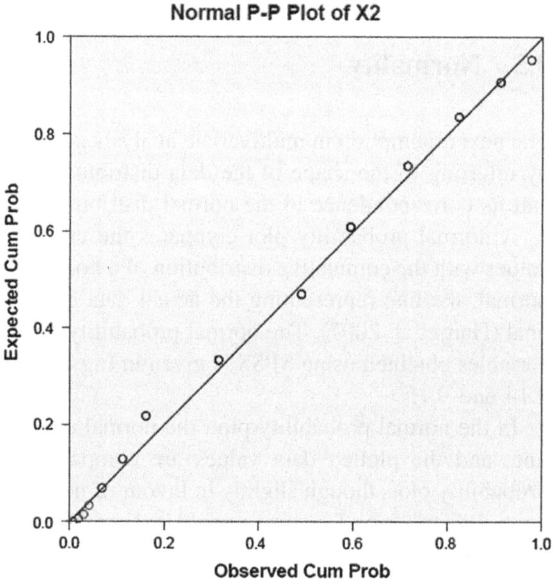

proceed further with prudence, since the regression analysis has been shown to be quite robust (Hair et al. 2007). This is further justified by the following reasons: Sample size has the effect of increasing statistical power by reducing sampling error. Hence, larger sample sizes reduce the detrimental effects of non-normality. In small samples of less than 30 or so, significant departures from normality can have

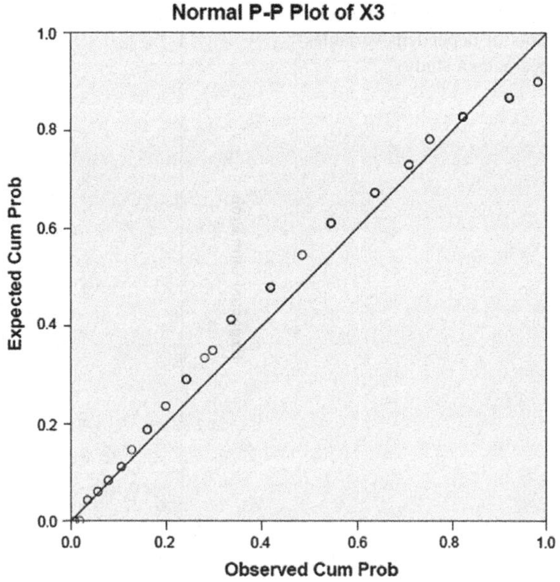

Fig. 9.9 Normal probability plots of independent variables (Tamil Nadu study)

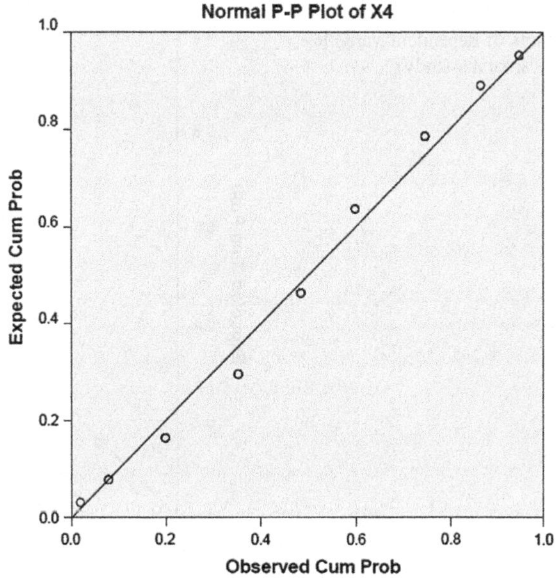

Fig. 9.10 Normal probability plots of independent variables (Tamil Nadu study)

substantial impact on the results (Hair et al. 2007). In the present research, the sample size is 91 for both Karnataka and Tamil Nadu study. Hence in most instances as the sample size becomes large; the analysis can be less concerned about

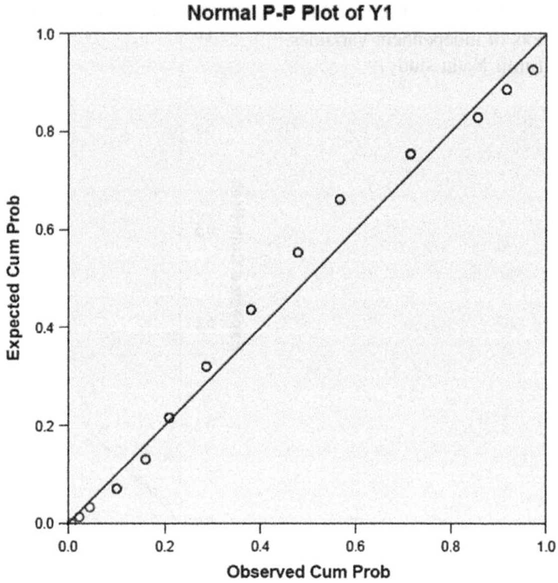

Fig. 9.11 Normal probability plots of dependent variables (Karnataka study)

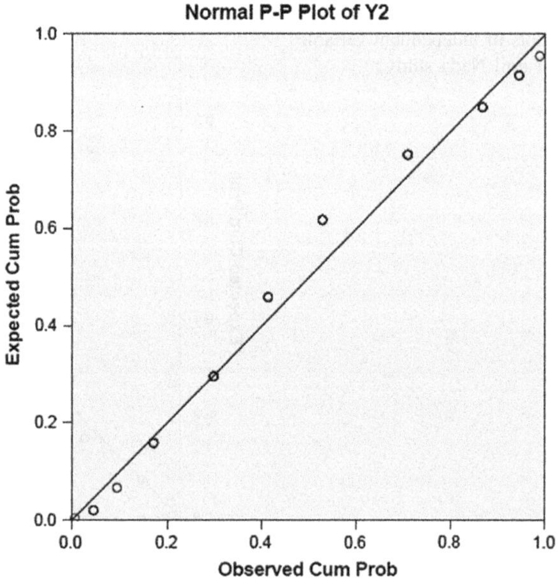

Fig. 9.12 Normal probability plots of dependent variables (Karnataka study)

non-normal variables, except as they might lead to other assumption violations that have an impact in other ways. Nevertheless, here in the current research the other assumption violations are not there.

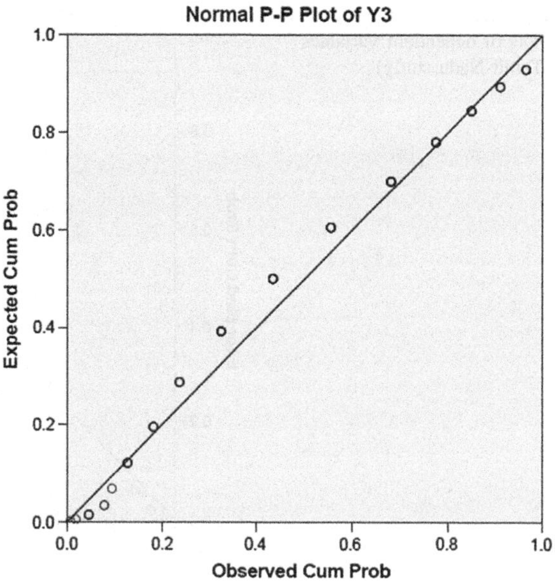

Fig. 9.13 Normal probability plots of dependent variables (Karnataka study)

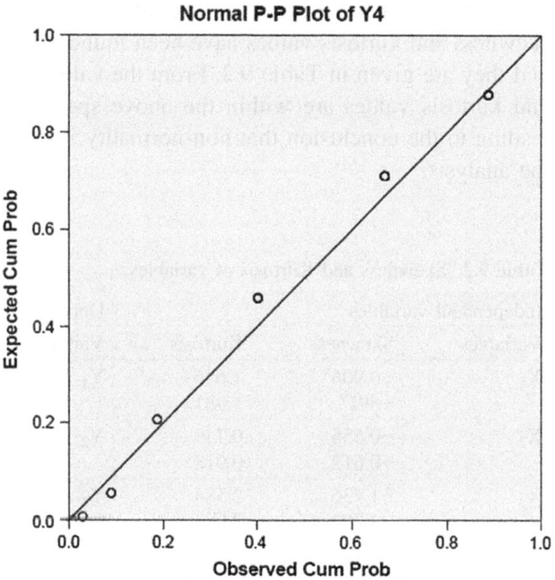

Fig. 9.14 Normal probability plots of dependent variables (Tamil Nadu study)

In addition, problems associated with non-normality depend on the values of skewness and kurtosis. Non-normality of variables unless skewness is severe (>±4 or ±5, maybe even larger) and kurtosis is severe (>3) and combinations of

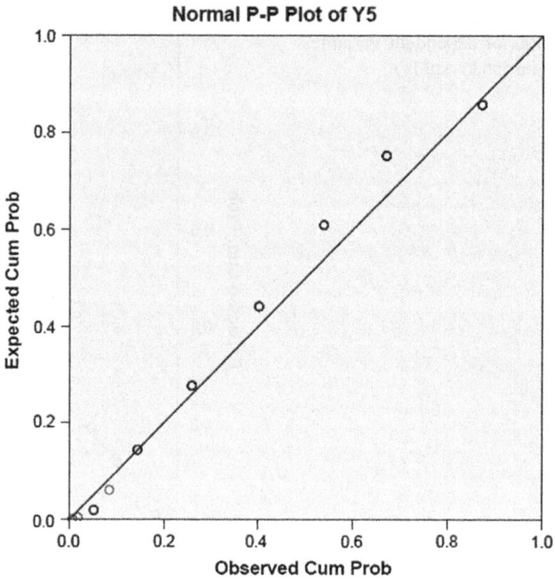

Fig. 9.15 Normal probability plots of dependent variables (Tamil Nadu study)

skewness and kurtosis at the edge of these values may cause problems. The skewness and kurtosis values have been found out using SPSS for all the variables and they are given in Table 9.2. From the values, it can be seen that the skewness and kurtosis values are within the above specification limits in both the studies leading to the conclusion that non-normality is not going to pose any problem for the analysis.

Table 9.2 Skewness and Kurtosis of variables

Independent variables			Dependent variables		
Variables	Skewness	Kurtosis	Variables	Skewness	Kurtosis
X_1	−0.906[a] −891[b]	1.646 1.981	Y_1	−0.450 −0.513	−0.364 −0.412
X_2	−0.556 −0.612	0.749 0.918	Y_2	−0.123 −0.213	−0.699 −0.712
X_3	−1.736 −1.892	2.584 2.981	Y_3	−0.482 −0.513	−0.153 −0.213
X_4	−0.178 −0.231	−0.917 −0.891	Y_4	−0.668 −0.712	0.371 0.413
			Y_5	−0.431 −0.512	−0.619 −0.712

[a]Karnataka study
[b]Tamil Nadu study

9.6 Estimating the Regression Model and Assessing the Overall Model Fit

With the regression analysis specified in terms of dependent and independent variables, the sample deemed adequate for the objectives of the study, and the assumptions assessed for the individual variables, the model building process now proceeds to the estimation of the regression model and assessing the overall model fit. Here three tasks are to be accomplished:

1. Selection of a method for specifying the regression model to be estimated.
2. Assessing the statistical significance of the overall model in predicting the dependent variable.
3. Determination of whether any of the observations exert an undue influence on the results.

9.7 Selection of a Method for Specifying the Regression Model to Be Estimated

Here the confirmatory regression model is adopted wherein we have specified the independent variables to be included in the regression equation. In this manner, the complete control over the regression variate in terms of both prediction and explanation is retained. Here theory is the guiding factor in evaluating the regression model. This approach is especially appropriate in situations for validation purposes (Hair et al. 2007).

The other approach of regression, a stepwise regression is also adopted for a cross verification in the interpretation stage of the regression model, mainly to capture the strengths of both these approaches.

Having already identified the independent variables to be included, it is required to find out the effect of all these independent variable on the overall relationship hypothesized. The full model involving all the variables i.e. each construct of innovation performance as the dependent variable (Y_1, Y_2, Y_3, Y_4 and Y_5) and the different Strategic Marketing constructs as the independent variables (X_1, X_2, X_3, and X_4) are given below:

Model 1

$Y_1 = b_{10} + b_{11}X_1 + b_{12}X_2 + b_{13}X_3 + b_{14}X_4 + u_1$

Model 2

$Y_2 = b_{20} + b_{21}X_1 + b_{22}X_2 + b_{23}X_3 + b_{24}X_4 + u_2$

Model 3

$Y_3 = b_{30} + b_{31}X_1 + b_{32}X_2 + b_{33}X_3 + b_{34}X_4 + u_3$

Model 4
$Y_4 = b_{40} + b_{41}X_1 + b_{42}X_2 + b_{43}X_3 + b_{44}X_4 + u_4$
Model 5
$Y_5 = b_{50} + b_{51}X_1 + b_{52}X_2 + b_{53}X_3 + b_{54}X_4 + u_5$

9.8 Assessing the Statistical Significance of the Overall Model in Predicting the Dependent Variable

Examining the statistical significance of the model involves two tests.

1. A test of the variation explained (coefficient of determination, R^2)
2. A test of each regression coefficient

R^2 value is a single measure of overall predictive accuracy representing the combined effect of the entire variate in prediction, even when the regression equation contains more than one independent variable. It is the squared correlation of the actual and predicted value. A more objective measure relating the level of over fitting to the R^2 achieved by the model is the adjusted R^2. This measure involves an adjustment based on the number of independent variables relative to the sample size. This is interpreted in the same manner as the unadjusted coefficient of determination. The adjusted R^2 decreases with fewer observations per independent variable (Hair et al. 2007).

Significance testing of the regression coefficient is statistically based probability estimate of, whether the estimated coefficients across the large number of samples of a certain size will indeed be different from zero. For making this judgment, three concepts are relied on:

1. Establishing the significance level (alpha), a typically used value being 0.05.
2. Sampling error, due to variation in sample sizes.
3. Standard error, the expected variation of the estimated coefficients due to sampling error.

The estimates of the multiple regression analysis carried for the collected data from 91 organizations using SPSS is given in Table 9.3a, b. The analysis indicates that all the models are reasonably good, leading to the rejection of the null hypothesis.

Multiple *R* is the correlation coefficient of the actual and the predicted value of the dependent variable. From Table 9.3a, b, it can be seen that this value for all the models are reasonably high, indicating the model fit.

R^2 indicates the percentage of total variation of the dependent variable explained by the regression model consisting of all the four independent variables. Here also it can be seen that this is reasonably high, indicating the good model fit. The standard error of the estimate can be viewed as the standard deviation of the prediction errors and becomes a measure to assess the absolute size of the prediction error.

Table 9.3 Models summary

Model	R	R^2	Adjusted R^2	Std. error of the estimate
(a) Karnataka study				
1	0.724	0.524	0.501	0.41732
2	0.696	0.484	0.456	0.45149
3	0.757	0.573	0.552	0.39124
4	0.616	0. 379	0.356	0.34110
5	0.648	0.419	0.398	0.39231
(b) Tamil Nadu study				
1	0.691	0.477	0.456	0.43150
2	0.721	0.519	0.501	0.49157
3	0.758	0.574	0.605	0.40187
4	0.634	0.401	0.398	0.38574
5	0.691	0.477	0.457	0.40251

The ANOVA analysis provides the statistical test for the overall model fit in terms of the F ratio. Table 9.4a, b gives the ANOVA ratio of all the models obtained using SPSS. It can be seen that all the models are statistically significant indicated by the *p*-values, that are very much lower than 0.05.

This leads to the rejection of the null hypothesis for all the models in both studies and is as follows

Model 1—Relationship of Technological innovation to SM
Ho: $b_{10} = b_{11} = b_{12} = b_{13} = b_{14} = 0$
and Ha: Not all b_i *values equal to zero*
Model 2—Relationship of Product innovation to SM
Ho: $b_{20} = b_{21} = b_{22} = b_{23} = b_{24} = 0$
and Ha: Not all b_i *values equal to zero*
Model 3—Relationship of Process innovation to SM
Ho: $b_{30} = b_{31} = b_{32} = b_{33} = b_{34} = 0$

Table 9.4 ANOVA ratio

Model	F statistic	*p*-value
(a) Karnataka study		
1	13.689	0.000
2	7.410	0.000
3	16.285	0.000
4	7.388	0.000
5	9.229	0.000
(b) Tamil Nadu study		
1	12.453	0.000
2	8.9122	0.000
3	13.413	0.000
4	8.5134	0.000
5	9.6712	0.000

and Ha: Not all b_i *values equal to zero*
Model 4—Relationship of System innovation to SM
Ho: $b_{40} = b_{41} = b_{42} = b_{43} = b_{44} = 0$
and Ha: Not all b_i *values equal to zero*
Model 5—Relationship of Innovation management to SM
Ho: $b_{50} = b_{51} = b_{52} = b_{53} = b_{54} = 0$
and Ha: Not all b_i *values equal to zero*

9.9 Determination of Outliers and Influential's

Here we shift our attention to individual observations, with the objective of finding observations that are:

1. Outliers—observations that lie outside the general patterns of the data set.
2. Influential observations—observations that strongly influence the regression results.

The degree to which outliers affect the regression solution depends upon where the outlier is located relative to the other cases in the analysis. Outliers whose location has a large effect on the regression solution are called influential cases.

Whether or not a case is influential is measured by Cook's distance (Kutner et al. 2005). Cook's distance measures the effect of deleting a given observation. Cook's distance is an index measure; it is compared to a critical value based on the formula:

Cook's Distance, C = 4 /(n − k − 1)

Where n is the number of cases and k is the number of independent variables. If a case has a Cook's distance greater than the critical value, it is to be examined for exclusion. Here in the current research:

Cook's Distance, C = 4/(91 − 4 − 1) = 0.046

A case may have a large influence on the regression analysis, resulting in an analysis that is less representative of the population represented by the sample. The criteria for identifying influential case is a Cook's distance score with a value of 0.046 or greater.

A score on the dependent variable is considered unusual if its studentized residual is bigger than ±3.0. The combination of scores for the independent variables is an outlier if the probability of the Mahalanobis D^2 distance score is less than or equal to 0.001 (Hair et al. 2007). Cases were selected based on the criteria of the Cook's distance, Mahalanobi's D^2 and studentised residual and cases requiring exclusion were identified using SPSS. Considering the studentised residual scores, probability of Mahalanobis D^2, critical value of Cook's distance, the following number of cases for each model were identified as valid resulting in the number of cases available for, noted against each model in Table 9.5a, b.

Once the outliers and influential cases are removed, it is needed to check the sample size requirement for regression. The minimum ratio of valid cases to independent variables for multiple regression is 5–1. From Table 9.5a, b, after removing influential cases and outliers, there are 81–90 valid cases (in both the

Table 9.5 Details of cases after removal of outliers and influential

Model	No. of valid cases	Ratio of valid cases to Independent variables
(a) Karnataka study		
1	84	21.00
2	89	22.25
3	90	22.50
4	89	22.25
5	88	22.00
(b) Tamil Nadu study		
1	81	20.25
2	87	21.75
3	88	22.00
4	85	21.25
5	89	22.25

studies) for each model and 4 independent variables. The minimum ratio of cases to independent variables for this analysis is 20.25 and this satisfies the minimum requirement.

9.10 Running the Regression Excluding Outliers and Influentials

The regression was executed again, without the outliers and influential cases. Table 9.6a, b gives the model summary after removal of outliers and influential cases obtained using SPSS.

Table 9.6 Model summary after removal of outliers and influential

Model	R	R^2	Adjusted R^2	Std. error of the estimate
(a) Karnataka study				
1	0.756	0.571	0.557	0.3988
2	0.781	0.609	0.589	0.4402
3	0.801	0.641	0.621	0.4704
4	0.710	0.504	0.501	0.2883
5	0.720	0.518	0.498	0.3208
(b) Tamil Nadu study				
1	0.728	0.529	0.0.507	0.4051
2	0.805	0.648	0.625	0.4687
3	0.798	0.636	0.602	0.4571
4	0.712	0.506	0.501	0.3875
5	0.768	0.589	0.527	0.3977

Prior to the removal of outliers and influential cases, the minimum proportion of variance among all the five models in the dependent variable explained by the independent variables (R^2) was 37.9 and 40.1% for Karnataka and Tamil Nadu studies respectively. After removing outliers and influential cases, the minimum proportion of variance among all the five models in the dependent variable explained by the independent variables (R^2) is 50.4 and 48.7% respectively for Karnataka and Tamil Nadu study.

The change in R^2 and the proportion of change in R^2 is given in Table 9.7a, b.

Since the regression analysis after omitting outliers and influential cases explained at least two percent more variance than the regression analysis with all cases and no transformations, the regression analysis with omitted outliers and influential cases was interpreted.

Table 9.8a, b shows the ANOVA ratio after removal of outliers and influential's obtained using SPSS. The probability of the F statistic for the overall regression relationship is <0.001, less than or equal to the level of significance of 0.05. Hence the null hypothesis of no relationship between the set of independent variables and the dependent variable is rejected ($R^2 = 0$). This supports the research hypothesis that there is a statistically significant relationship between the set of independent variables and the dependent variable.

Regarding multiple R for the relationship between the set of independent variables and the dependent variable, using the rule of thumb that a correlation less than or equal to 0.20 is characterized as very weak; greater than 0.20 and less than or equal to 0.40 is weak; greater than 0.40 and less than or equal to 0.60 is moderate; greater than 0.60 and less than or equal to 0.80 is strong; and greater than 0.80 is very strong. These relationships are discussed in detail in chapter on Discussions and conclusions. The type of relationship between dependent and independent variables is given in Table 9.9a, b.

Table 9.7 Change in R^2 after eliminating outliers and influential cases

Model	R^2 prior to removal of outliers and influential's	R^2 after to removal of outliers and influential's	Change in R^2 percentage
(a) Karnataka study			
1	0.524	0.571	8.96
2	0.484	0.609	25.82
3	0.573	0.641	11.86
4	0. 379	0.504	32.98
5	0.419	0.518	23.62
(b) Tamil Nadu study			
1	0.477	0.529	10.9
2	0.519	0.648	24.85
3	0.574	0.636	10.8
4	0.401	0.506	26.18
5	0.477	0.589	23.48

Table 9.8 ANOVA Ratio after removal of outliers and influential

Model	F statistic	*p*-value
(a) Karnataka study		
1	15.101	0.000
2	9.071	0.000
3	19.312	0.000
4	9.402	0.000
5	11.314	0.000
(b) Tamil Nadu study		
1	13.344	0.000
2	8.913	0.000
3	21.125	0.000
4	9.918	0.000
5	12.012	0.000

Table 9.9 Type of relationship between variables

Model	Multiple R	Type of relationship
(a) Karnataka study		
1	0.756	Strong
2	0.781	Strong
3	0.801	Very strong
4	0.710	Strong
5	0.720	Strong
(b) Tamil Nadu study		
1	0.728	Strong
2	0.805	Very strong
3	0.798	Strong
4	0.698	Strong
5	0.768	Strong

9.11 Evaluating the Variate for the Assumptions of Regression Analysis

Meeting the assumptions of regression analysis for the individual variables has been examined. However, it is also required to evaluate the variate for meeting these assumptions as well. The assumptions to examine are linearity, normality, homoscedasticity, independence of the residuals and multicollinearity. The principle used in evaluating the regression variate is the residual analysis (Hair et al. 2007).

The principal measure of the prediction error for the variate is the residual—the difference between the observed and the predicted value of the dependent variable. The most widely used is the studentized residual whose values correspond to the *t* values. Plotting the residuals versus the independent predicted variables is a basic method for identifying the assumption violations for the overall relationship.

Violation of each assumption can be identified by specific patterns of the residuals. All assumptions are met, when residuals fall randomly with relatively equal dispersion about zero and no pattern is found for large versus small values (Hair et al. 2007).

9.11.1 Linearity

Linearity of any bivariate relationship is examined through residual plots. Typical non-random pattern of residuals indicate existence of non-liner relationships. Linearity is assessed through an analysis of residuals, testing the overall variate for all the five models. The residual plots obtained using SPSS is given in Figs. 9.16, 9.17, 9.18, 9.19 and 9.20 for the models. The plots does not exhibit any non linear pattern to the residuals thus ensuring the overall equation is linear.

The similar plots were obtained for the Tamil Nadu study and they are also acceptable as similar to that of Karnataka study.

9.11.2 Homoscedasticity

The next assumption deals with the constancy of residuals across values of the independent variables. Diagnosis of homoscedasticity is made with residual plots or simple statistical tests. Plotting the residuals against the predicted dependent values and absence of any consistent pattern in this plot indicates homoscedasticity. Again, the residual plots given in Figs. 9.16, 9.17, 9.18, 9.19 and 9.20 do not show pattern of increasing or decreasing residuals. This finding indicates homoscedasticity in the multivariate case. Statistical tests to diagnose homoscedasticity also have been

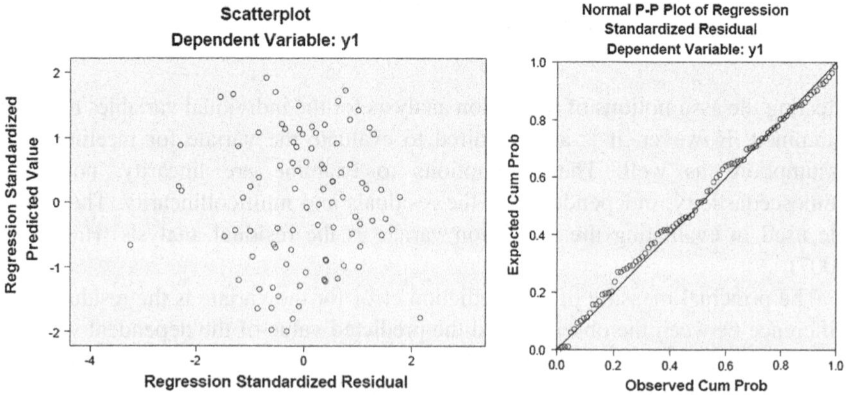

Fig. 9.16 Model 1—Residuals—scatter plot and normal P-P plot (Karnataka study)

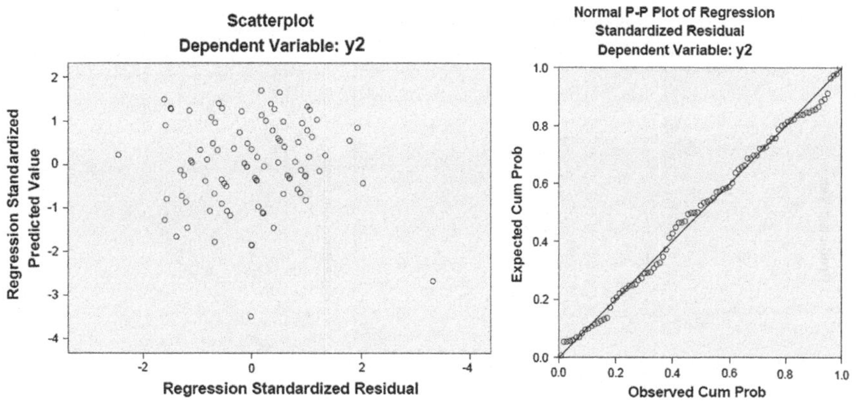

Fig. 9.17 Model 2—Residuals—scatter plot and normal P-P plot (Karnataka study)

carried out. The Levene's test of homogeneity of variances has been carried out using SPSS for the groups of variables as given in Table 9.10a, b.

The null hypothesis for the test of homogeneity of variance states that the variance of the dependent variable is equal across groups defined by the independent variable, i.e., the variance is homogeneous. The above significance values given in Table 9.10a, b indicate that, the probability associated with the Levene Statistic for almost all pairs of variables is greater than the level of significance, 0.05. Here we do not reject the null hypothesis and conclude that the variance is homogeneous.

9.11.3 Normality

The next assumption to check is the normality of the error term of the variate with a visual examination of the normal probability plots of residuals. As can be seen from the normal probability plots (Normal PP Plots) obtained using SPSS, in Figs. 9.16, 9.17, 9.18, 9.19 and 9.20 the values fall along the diagonal with no substantial or systematic departures. Thus, the residuals are considered to represent a normal distribution. This is further verified by the Shapiro Wilks normality test as given in Table 9.11a, b obtaincd using SPSS for all the error terms for the five models.

From the Table 9.11 it can be seen that all the p-values are greater than 0.05 wherein the null hypothesis of normality cannot be rejected.

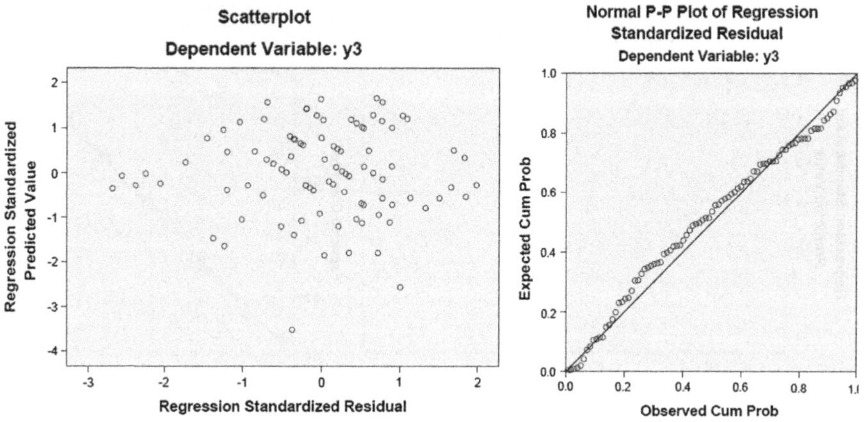

Fig. 9.18 Model 3—Residuals—scatter plot and normal P-P plot (Karnataka study)

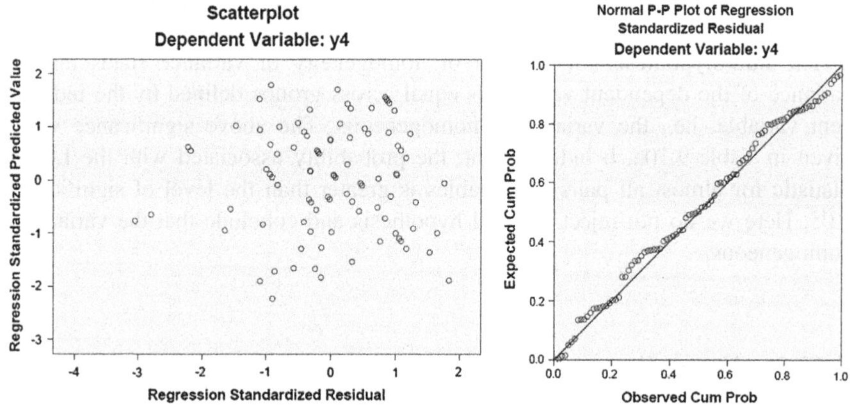

Fig. 9.19 Model 4—Residuals—scatter plot and normal P-P plot (Karnataka study)

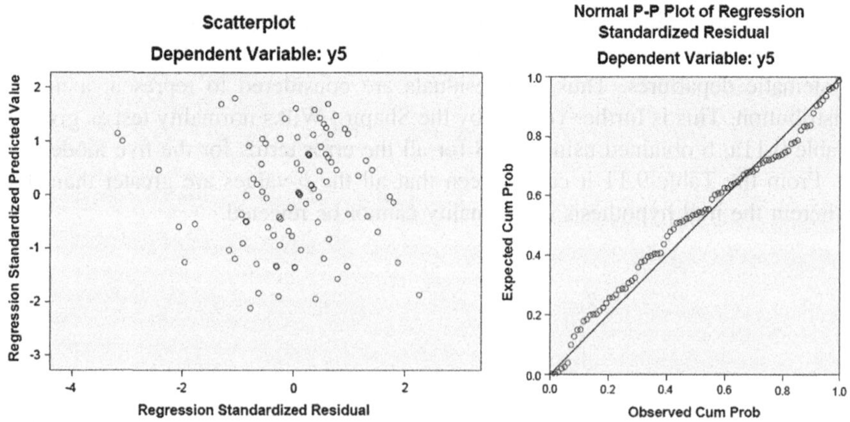

Fig. 9.20 Model 5—Residuals—scatter plot and normal P-P plot (Karnataka study)

Table 9.10 Significance for Levene's test of homogeneity of variances

	X_1	X_2	X_3	X_4
(a) Karnataka study				
u_1	0.444	0.831	0.077	0.803
u_2	0.330	0.232	0.052	0.051
u_3	0.230	0.230	0.088	0.552
u_4	0.437	0.590	0.376	0.772
u_5	0.968	0.726	0.407	0.789
(b) Tamil Nadu study				
u_1	0.393	0.791	0.065	0.798
u_2	0.431	0.301	0.059	0.061
u_3	0.321	0.278	0.079	0.601
u_4	0.510	0.603	0.456	0.810
u_5	0.891	0.805	0.396	0.845

Table 9.11 Shapiro-Wilks normality test of Residuals (Karnataka study)

Models	1	2	3	4	5
(a) Karnataka study					
p-value ($p > 0.05$)	0.3254	0.3442	0.2850	0.1296	0.1154
(b) Tamil Nadu study					
p-value ($p > 0.05$)	0.4123	0.2981	0.3015	0.2033	0.1574

9.12 Measuring the Degree and Impact of Multicolinearity

Multicollinearity occurs when one independent variable is so strongly correlated with one or more other variables that its relationship to the dependent variable is likely to be misinterpreted. Its potential unique contribution to explaining the dependent variable is minimized by its strong relationship to other independent variables.

A key issue in interpreting the regression variate is the correlation among the independent variables. The ideal situation would be to have a number of independent variables highly correlated with the dependent variable, but with little correlation among them. In any interpretation of the regression variate, awareness is required on the impact of multicolinearity. Highly collinear variables can distort the results substantially or make them quite unstable and thus not generalisable. The Variance Inflation factor (VIF) is one measure available to test the impact of multicolinearity. Any variable with tolerance values below 0.10 meaning a VIF of more than 10 would have a correlation more than 0.95 indicating high

Table 9.12 Variance inflation factor

Variable	Model 1	Model 2	Model 3	Model 4	Model 5
(a) Karnataka study					
X_1	1.980	1.979	2.012	2.211	2.015
X_2	2.136	2.158	2.245	2.347	2.211
X_3	1.937	1.943	1.998	1.957	1.977
X_4	1.524	1.524	1.614	1.601	1.651
(b) Tamil Nadu study					
X_1	2.1011	2.451	1.982	2.452	2.987
X_2	2.763	1.985	2.897	2.542	1.997
X_3	2.045	1.876	2.078	2.034	1.876
X_4	1.785	1.998	1.753	1.599	1.789

multicollinearity. A common cut off threshold is a tolerance value of 0.10, which corresponds to a VIF value of 10 (Hair et al. 2007). Multicollinearity is indicated when the VIF value for an independent variable is greater than 10.

The values of variance inflation factor obtained using SPSS for the independent variables in the current research is less than 10 as given in Table 9.12a, b.This indicates absence of multicollinearity. The variance inflation factor values for all of the independent variables in all the five models in both the study is less than 10. Hence, multicollinearity is not a problem in this analysis.

9.13 Independence of Residuals

Violation of this assumption affects the precision of the estimates but not the accuracy of the estimates. i.e. estimates remains unbiased and the variances become underestimated. One method of detection of this auto correlation or independence of residuals is the Durbin-Watson Statistic, D. The value of D lies between zero and 4 ($0 < D < 4$), and a value of $D \approx 2$, (i.e., $1.5 < D < 2.5$) indicates no autocorrelation. Table 9.13a, b gives the values of Durbin Watson statistic for all the models obtained using SPSS.

Table 9.13 Autocorrelation—Durbin Watson

Model	1	2	3	4	5
(a) Karnataka study					
Durbin Watson Statistic	2.061	2.188	2.026	2.298	2.030
(b) Tamil Nadu study					
Durbin Watson Statistic	2.321	2.211	2.103	2.415	2.001

Table 9.14 Summary of assumptions of regression analysis

Assumptions and Conditions	Regression models				
	1	2	3	4	5
(a) Karnataka study					
Ratio of cases to IV > 5	21.0	22.25	22.50	22.25	22.0
ANOVA significance < 0.05	0.000	0.000	0.000	0.000	0.000
Absence of non linear patterns	OK	OK	OK	OK	OK
Residual normality ($p > 0.05$)	0.3254	0.3442	0.2850	0.1296	0.1154
Homoscedasticity ($p > 0.05$)	0.0770	0.0500	0.0880	0.376	0.407
Multicollinearity (VIF < 10)	2.136	2.158	2.245	2.347	2.211
Autocorrelation (DW $\approx$ 2.0)	2.061	2.188	2.026	2.298	2.030
$R^2 > 0.5$	0.571	0.609	0.641	0.504	0.518
Model adequacy	OK	OK	OK	OK	OK
(b) Tamil Nadu study					
Ratio of cases to IV > 5	20.25	21.75	22.00	21.25	22.25
ANOVA significance < 0.05	0.000	0.000	0.000	0.000	0.000
Absence of non linear patterns	OK	OK	OK	OK	OK
Residual normality ($p > 0.05$)	0.4123	0.2981	0.3015	0.2033	0.1574
Homoscedasticity ($p > 0.05$)	0.065	0.059	0.079	0.456	0.396
Multicollinearity (VIF < 10)	2.763	1.985	2.897	2.542	1.995
Autocorrelation (DW $\approx$ 2.0)	2.321	2.211	2.103	2.415	2.003
$R^2 > 0.5$	0.529	0.648	0.636	0.506	0.589
Model adequacy	OK	OK	OK	OK	OK

It can be seen that the Durbin Watson statistic for all the models are within the specified values indicating the independence of residuals.

9.14 Summary of Assumptions and Model Fits

The variate has been evaluated for the assumptions of regression analysis. This is summarized in the form of a Table 9.14a, b. From the table it can be seen that there is an overall model fit and the models could be interpreted based on the coefficients.

The final regression coefficients for all the five models obtained using SPSS are discussed in detail and interpreted in the next chapter. Both confirmatory and stepwise approaches are employed in regression analysis to capture the strengths of each by the statistical significance obtained. The next chapter gives a detailed discussion on the interpretation of these regression models based on the coefficients.

9.15 Review Questions

1. Explain the assumptions made in multiple regression analysis.
2. Explain the concept of Linearity, Normality and Homoscedasticity used in the analysis.
3. What is skewness and kurtosis of variables?
4. Explain the two tests done to examine the significance of the model.

References

Hair JF Jr, Black WC, Babin BJ, Anderson RE, Tatham RL (2007) Multivariate data analysis, 6th edn. Pearson Prentice Hall (Chap. 1, 2 & 4)

Kutner MH, Nachtsheim CJ, Neter J, Li W (2005) Applied linear statistical models, 5th edn. Mc Graw Hill

Chapter 10
Results and Discussion

Abstract The regression models were estimated in the previous chapter. The regression variate was specified and the diagnostic tests that confirm the appropriateness and the assumptions underlying the regression models were administered. In this chapter, we examine the predictive equation based on four independent variables and five dependent variables. The regression coefficients become indicators of the relative impact and importance of the independent variables (Strategic Marketing) in their relationship with the dependent variable (Innovation performance). The final task in multiple regression is the validation process of the regression model. The primary concern of this process is to ensure that the results are generalisable to the population and not specific to the sample used in estimation. Here in our research the split sample validation process is adopted for the models validation and followed by the final conclusion regarding the study made with respect to both Karnataka and Tamil Nadu.

The key takeaways for the reader from this chapter are listed below

1. Interpreting the regression variate and coefficient.
2. The predictive equation for models based on the confirmatory approach.
3. Overview of results and its validation.
4. Conclusion and important findings of this study.
5. Limitations of this study and directions for future research.

Keywords Regression variate · Regression coefficient · Predictive equation · Confirmatory estimation approach · Standardized coefficient

10.1 Explanation with Multiple Regression

Multiple regression provides a means of objectively assessing the degree and character of the relationship between dependent and independent variables. It is accomplished by forming the variate of independent variables and then examining

R. Srinivasan and C.P. Lohith, *Strategic Marketing and Innovation for Indian MSMEs*, India Studies in Business and Economics,
DOI 10.1007/978-981-10-3590-6_10

the magnitude, sign, and statistical significance of the regression coefficient for each independent variable. In this manner, the independent variables can be considered for their individual contribution to the variate and its explanations. Interpretation of the variate may rely on any of the three perspectives:

1. The importance of the independent variables.
2. The types of relationships found
3. The interrelationship among the independent variables.

The most direct interpretation of the regression variate is the determination of the relative importance of each independent variable in the explanation of the dependent measure. Multiple regression analysis provides a means of objectively assessing the magnitude and direction (positive or negative) of each independent variables relationship. In addition to assessing the importance of each variable, multiple regression also provides a means of assessing the nature of the relationships between the independent variable and the dependent variable. Finally, multiple regression provides insight into the relationships among independent variables in their prediction of the dependent measure, which are needed for explanation purpose.

The confirmatory approach adopted in the present research provides a control over the regression variate, but at the possible cost of a regression equation with lower prediction and explanation. Since both the confirmatory and the stepwise approaches have strengths and weaknesses, both methods are employed in order to capture the strengths of each by the statistical significance obtained.

10.2 Interpreting the Regression Variate and Coefficient

The next step is the interpretation of the regression variate by evaluating the estimated regression coefficients for their explanation of the dependent variable. The estimated regression coefficients termed the *B* coefficients represent both the type of relationship (positive or negative) and the strength of the relationship between independent and dependent variables in the regression variate. For explanatory purposes, the regression coefficients become indicators of the relative impact and importance of the independent variables in their relationship with the dependent variable.

In order to use the regression coefficients for explanatory purpose it is required to ensure that all of the independent variables are on comparable scales. The objective of comparing the independent variables in scale and variability is achieved by using a modified regression coefficient called the beta coefficient.

When all the variables are expressed in a standardized scale, then the regression coefficients represent relative importance. Here beta weight is the preferred measure of the relative importance. Beta coefficients eliminate the problem of dealing with

Table 10.1 Variables of Strategic Marketing (SM) and innovation performance

Independent variables of strategic marketing		Dependent variables of innovation performance	
Environmental landscaping	X_1	Technological innovation	Y_1
Marketing mix	X_2	Product innovation	Y_2
Brand positioning	X_3	Process innovation	Y_3
Entrepreneurial management	X_4	System innovation	Y_4
		Innovation management	Y_5

different units of measurement. They thus reflect the relative impact on the dependent variable of a change in one standard deviation in either variable. This is a common unit of measurement, which could be used for determining which variable has the most impact.

The regression models were estimated in the previous chapter. The regression variate was specified and the diagnostic tests that confirm the appropriateness and the assumptions underlying the regression models were administered. In this chapter, we examine the predictive equation based on four independent variables and five dependent variables. Table 10.1 lists the respective variables.

The predictive equation for models based on the confirmatory approach for the both the study follows:

Model 1

$Y_1 = (0.405) + 0.081\ X_1 + 0.223\ X_2 + 0.017\ X_3 + 0.555\ X_4$

$Y_1 = (0.395) + 0.077\ X_1 + 0.246\ X_2 + 0.013\ X_3 + 0.456\ X_4$

Model 2

$Y_2 = (1.246) + 0.048\ X_1 + 0.142\ X_2 + 0.193\ X_3 + 0.254\ X_4$

$Y_2 = (1.323) + 0.055\ X_1 + 0.252\ X_2 + 0.201\ X_3 + 0.303\ X_4$

Model 3

$Y_3 = (0.610) + 0.164\ X_1 + 0.186\ X_2 + 0.190\ X_3 + 0.309\ X_4$

$Y_3 = (0.597) + 0.210\ X_1 + 0.199\ X_2 + 0.204\ X_3 + 0.299\ X_4$

Model 4

$Y_4 = (2.232) + 0.182\ X_1 + (-0.024)\ X_2 + 0.033\ X_3 + 0.316\ X_4$

$Y_4 = (1.998) + 0.177\ X_1 + (-0.036)\ X_2 + 0.056\ X_3 + 0.412\ X_4$

Model 5

$Y_5 = (1.474) + 0.125\ X_1 + 0.082\ X_2 + 0.045\ X_3 + 0.0418\ X_4$

$Y_5 = (1.567) + 0.167\ X_1 + 0.098\ X_2 + 0.053\ X_3 + 0.0399\ X_4$

It is conceptually impossible for observations to exist with all the independent variables measured at zero. Hence, the constant term is outside the data and acts only to position the model. In this research the intercept has no explanatory value because in no instances do all independent variables have values of zero. All the above models are discussed in detail in the subsequent sections.

10.3 MODEL 1—Strategic Marketing and Technological Innovation

Summary of the regression coefficients and significance with respect to model 1 for both the study, through the confirmatory estimation approach and the stepwise estimation approach is given in Tables 10.2a, b and 10.3a, b respectively.

Karnataka study

From the confirmatory approach, it can be seen that two variables X_2 and X_4 is statistically significant ($p \leq 0.1$), whereas the stepwise model also contains two significant ($p \leq 0.05$) variables X_2 and X_4.

Hence, in the current research we consider Marketing Mix (X_2) and Entrepreneurial Management (X_4) are the variables that have a direct impact on Technological innovation performance (Y_1). Moreover, the non-significance of all variables other than Entrepreneurial management (X_4) and Marketing Mix (X_2) is leading to the conclusion that the other variables are not having a direct impact on Technological innovation performance (Y_1).

In viewing the regression coefficient of the significant variables the sign is an indication of the relationship (positive or negative) between the independent and dependent variables. The significant variables, Marketing Mix (X_2) and Entrepreneurial Management (X_4) has positive coefficients. This indicates that more positive perceptions of SM, i.e. higher values of Marketing Mix (X_2) and Entrepreneurial Management (X_4) increases Technological innovation performance (Y_1).

The beta coefficients are listed in the column headed standardized coefficients beta, which could be used for direct comparison. On direct comparison, it can be seen that the variables Marketing Mix (X_2) and Entrepreneurial management (X_4) are important for Technological innovation performance. However, relative

Table 10.2 Model 1—coefficients

Karnataka study						
Model 1	Coefficients	Unstandardized coefficients B	Std. error	Standardized coefficients beta	T	Sig.
(a) Confirmatory estimation approach						
Dependent variable Y_1	Constants	0.405	0.512		0.792	0.431
	X_1	0.081	0.138	0.069	0.586	0.560
	X_2	0.223	0.134	0.205	1.663	0.100
	X_3	0.017	0.096	0.021	0.175	0.861
	X_4	0.555	0.130	0.442	4.252	0.000
(b) Stepwise estimation approach						
Dependent variable Y_1	(Constant)	0.469	0.493		0.952	0.344
	X_2	0.270	0.101	0.248	2.671	0.009
	X_4	0.591	0.116	0.472	5.085	0.000

Table 10.3 Model 1—coefficients

Tamil Nadu study						
Model 1	Coefficients	Unstandardized coefficients B	Std. error	Standardized coefficients beta	T	Sig.
(a) Confirmatory estimation approach						
Dependent variable Y_1	Constants	0.395	0.499		0.823	0.402
	X_1	0.077	0.125	0.061	0.645	0.525
	X_2	0.246	0.156	0.199	1.599	0.103
	X_3	0.013	0.089	0.0332	0.189	0.799
	X_4	0.456	0.142	0.489	3.897	0.000
(b) Stepwise estimation approach						
Dependent Variable Y_1	(Constant)	0.415	0.502		0.897	0.401
	X_2	0.269	0.101	0.248	2.671	0.009
	X_4	0.585	0.116	0.472	5.085	0.000

magnitudes indicate that Entrepreneurial Management (X_4) has a more marked effect than the other variable. Thus to the extent that Entrepreneurial management performed in a much better way than the other variables of SM, represents the most direct way of increasing Technological innovation performance.

Tamil Nadu study

From the confirmatory approach, it can be seen that a variable X_4 is statistically significant ($p \leq 0.1$), whereas the stepwise model also contains two significant ($p \leq 0.05$) variables X_2 and X_4.

Hence, in the current research we consider Entrepreneurial Management (X_4) is the variable that have a direct impact on Technological innovation performance (Y_1). Moreover, the non-significance of all variables other than Marketing Mix (X_2) is leading to the conclusion that the other variables are not having a direct impact on Technological innovation performance (Y_1) with respect to Tamil Nadu study.

In viewing the regression coefficient of the significant variables the sign is an indication of the relationship (positive or negative) between the independent and dependent variables. The significant variable Entrepreneurial Management (X_4) has positive coefficients. This indicates that more positive perceptions of SM, i.e. higher values of Entrepreneurial Management (X_4) increases Technological innovation performance (Y_1).

The beta coefficients are listed in the column headed standardized coefficients beta, which could be used for direct comparison. On direct comparison, it can be seen that the variable Entrepreneurial management (X_4) is important for Technological innovation performance. Thus to the extent that Entrepreneurial management performed in a much better way than the other variables of SM, represents the most direct way of increasing Technological innovation performance.

10.4 MODEL 2—Strategic Marketing and Product Innovation

Summary of the regression coefficients and significance with respect to model 2, through the confirmatory estimation approach and the stepwise estimation approach for both the study is given in Tables 10.4 and 10.5 respectively.

Karnataka study

From the confirmatory approach, it can be seen that three variables $X_{2,}$ X_3 and X_4 are statistically significant ($p \leq 0.10$), whereas the stepwise model contains two significant ($p \leq 0.05$) variables X_3 and X_4.

Hence, in the current research we consider Marketing Mix (X_2), Brand Positioning (X_3) and Entrepreneurial Management (X_4) are the variables that have a direct impact on Product innovation performance (Y_2). Moreover, the non-significance of all variables other than Marketing Mix (X_2), Brand positioning (X_3) and Entrepreneurial management (X_4) is leading to the conclusion that the other variable is not having a direct impact on Product innovation performance (Y_2).

In viewing the regression coefficient of the significant variables the sign is an indication of the relationship (positive or negative) between the independent and dependent variables. The variables Marketing Mix (X_2), Brand Positioning (X_3) and Entrepreneurial Management (X_4) have a positive coefficient. This indicates that more positive perceptions of SM, i.e. higher values of Marketing Mix (X_2), Brand Positioning (X_3) and Entrepreneurial Management (X_4) increase Product innovation performance (Y_2).

The beta coefficients are listed in the column headed standardized coefficients beta, which could be used for direct comparison. On direct comparison, it can be seen that Brand positioning (X_3) is the most important. Moreover, relative magnitudes indicate that Marketing Mix (X_2) and Brand positioning (X_3) has a more marked effect than the other variable. Thus to the extent that Marketing Mix (X_2)

Table 10.4 Model 2—coefficients

Karnataka study						
Model 2	Coefficients	Unstandardized coefficients B	Std. error	Standardized coefficients beta	T	Sig.
(a) Confirmatory estimation approach						
Dependent variable Y_2	Constants	1.246	0.554		2.250	0.027
	X_1	0.048	0.149	0.042	0.323	0.748
	X_2	0.142	0.145	0.233	0.979	0.033
	X_3	0.193	0.104	0.240	1.855	0.067
	X_4	0.254	0.141	0.206	1.799	0.076
(b) Stepwise estimation approach						
Dependent variable Y_2	(Constant)	1.495	0.506		2.958	0.04
	X_3	0.268	0.082	0.334	3.261	0.002
	X_4	0.305	0.126	0.228	2.425	0.027

Table 10.5 Model 2—coefficients

Tamil Nadu study						
Model 2	Coefficients	Unstandardized coefficients B	Std. error	Standardized coefficients beta	T	Sig.
(a) Confirmatory estimation approach						
Dependent variable Y_2	Constants	1.323	0.502		2.025	0.025
	X_1	0.055	0.153	0.040	0.415	0.799
	X_2	0.252	0.165	0.256	0.998	0.045
	X_3	0.201	0.112	0.248	1.799	0.077
	X_4	0.303	0.158	0.278	1.854	0.084
(b) Stepwise estimation approach						
Dependent variable Y_2	(Constant)	1.405	0.545		2.758	0.05
	X_3	0.335	0.079	0.302	3.112	0.003
	X_4	0.299	0.148	0.235	2.299	0.045

and Brand positioning (X_3) activities performed in a much better way than the other variables of SM, represents the most direct way of increasing Product innovation performance (Y_2).

Tamil Nadu study

Summary of the regression coefficients and significance with respect to model 2, through the confirmatory estimation approach and the stepwise estimation approach is given in Table 10.5a, b respectively.

From the confirmatory approach, it can be seen that three variables X_2, X_3 and X_4 are statistically significant ($p \leq 0.10$), whereas the stepwise model contains two significant ($p \leq 0.05$) variables X_3 and X_4.

Hence, in the current study (Tamil Nadu) we also consider Marketing Mix (X_2), Brand Positioning (X_3) and Entrepreneurial Management (X_4) are the variables that have a direct impact on Product innovation performance (Y_2). Moreover, the non-significance of all variables other than Marketing Mix (X_2), Brand positioning (X_3) and Entrepreneurial management (X_4) is leading to the conclusion that the other variable is not having a direct impact on Product innovation performance (Y_2).

In viewing the regression coefficient of the significant variables the sign is an indication of the relationship (positive or negative) between the independent and dependent variables. The variables Marketing Mix (X_2), Brand Positioning (X_3) and Entrepreneurial Management (X_4) have a positive coefficient. This indicates that more positive perceptions of SM, i.e. higher values of Marketing Mix (X_2), Brand Positioning (X_3) and Entrepreneurial Management (X_4) increase Product innovation performance (Y_2).

The beta coefficients are listed in the column headed standardized coefficients beta, which could be used for direct comparison. On direct comparison, it can be seen that Brand positioning (X_3) is the most important. Moreover, relative magnitudes indicate that Marketing Mix (X_2) and Brand positioning (X_3) has a more marked effect than the other variable. Thus to the extent that Marketing Mix (X_2) and Brand positioning (X_3) activities performed in a much better way than the other variables of SM, represents the most direct way of increasing Product innovation performance (Y_2).

Inference: The result obtained for the Model 2 in both the studies are same.

10.5 MODEL 3—Strategic Marketing and Process Innovation

Summary of the regression coefficients and significance with respect to model 3, through the confirmatory estimation approach and the stepwise estimation approach are given in Tables 10.6 and 10.7 for both the studies respectively.

Karnataka study

From the confirmatory approach, it can be seen that two variables X_3 and X_4 are statistically significant ($p \leq 0.05$). The stepwise model contains the three significant ($p \leq 0.05$) variables X_2, X_3 and X_4.

The variable X_2 is non-significant in the confirmatory model and the impact of this variable is less certain. Hence in the current research we consider X_3 (Brand Positioning) and X_4 (Entrepreneurial Management) as the variables which have direct impact on Process innovation performance (Y_3). Moreover, the non-significance of all variables other than Brand Positioning (X_3) and Entrepreneurial management (X_4) is leading to the conclusion that the other variables are not having a direct impact on Product innovation performance (Y_3).

In viewing the regression coefficient of the significant variables the sign is an indication of the relationship (positive or negative) between the independent and dependent variables. All the two variables, Brand Positioning (X_3) and Entrepreneurial management (X_4) have positive coefficients. This indicates that

Table 10.6 Model 3—coefficients

Karnataka study						
Model 3	Coefficients	Unstandardized coefficients B	Std. error	Standardized coefficients beta	T	Sig.
(a) Confirmatory estimation approach						
Dependent variable Y_3	Constants	0.610	0.480		1.272	0.207
	X_1	0.164	0.129	0.145	1.270	0.208
	X_2	0.186	0.126	0.176	1.482	0.142
	X_3	0.190	0.090	0.239	2.111	0.058
	X_4	0.309	0.122	0.254	2.527	0.013
(b) Stepwise estimation approach						
Dependent variable Y_3	(Constant)	0.752	0.468		1.607	0.112
	X_2	0.239	0.119	0.226	2.008	0.048
	X_3	0.209	0.089	0.263	2.350	0.021
	X_4	0.370	0.113	0.304	3.284	0.001

Table 10.7 Model 3—coefficients

Tamil Nadu study						
Model 3	Coefficients	Unstandardized coefficients B	Std. error	Standardized coefficients beta	T	Sig.
(a) Confirmatory estimation approach						
Dependent variable Y_3	Constants	0.597	0.465		1.303	0.199
	X_1	0.210	0.136	0.139	1.361	0.312
	X_2	0.199	0.154	0.165	1.552	0.115
	X_3	0.204	0.087	0.241	2.056	0.041
	X_4	0.299	0.142	0.263	2.698	0.029
(b) Stepwise estimation approach						
Dependent variable Y_3	(Constant)	0.697	0.554		1.599	0.156
	X_2	0.321	0.123	0.229	2.234	0.033
	X_3	0.245	0.077	0.289	2.110	0.041
	X_4	0.402	0.125	0.335	3.456	0.022

more positive perceptions of SM, i.e. higher values Brand Positioning (X_3) and Entrepreneurial management (X_4) increase Process innovation performance (Y_3).

The beta coefficients are listed in the column headed standardized coefficients beta, which could be used for direct comparison. On direct comparison, it can be seen that Brand Positioning (X_3) and Entrepreneurial management (X_4) are more or less equally important variables for Process innovation performance (Y_3). Moreover, relative magnitudes indicate that both Brand Positioning (X_3) and Entrepreneurial management (X_4) have more marked effects than other variables. Thus to the extent that Brand Positioning activities and Entrepreneurial management activities are performed in a much better way than the other variables of SM, represents the most direct way of increasing Process innovation performance (Y_3).

Tamil Nadu study

From the confirmatory approach, it can be seen that, here in Tamil Nadu study also, two variables X_3 and X_4 are statistically significant ($p \leq 0.05$) and the stepwise model contains the three significant ($p \leq 0.05$) variables X_2, X_3 and X_4.

The variable X_2 is non-significant in the confirmatory model and the impact of this variable is less certain. Hence in the current research we consider X_3 (Brand Positioning) and X_4 (Entrepreneurial Management) as the variables which have direct impact on Process innovation performance (Y_3). Moreover, the non-significance of all variables other than Brand Positioning (X_3) and Entrepreneurial management (X_4) is leading to the conclusion that the other variables are not having a direct impact on Product innovation performance (Y_3).

In viewing the regression coefficient of the significant variables the sign is an indication of the relationship (positive or negative) between the independent and dependent variables. All the two variables, Brand Positioning (X_3) and Entrepreneurial management (X_4) have positive coefficients. This indicates that more positive perceptions of SM, i.e. higher values Brand Positioning (X_3) and Entrepreneurial management (X_4) increase Process innovation performance (Y_3).

The beta coefficients are listed in the column headed standardized coefficients beta, which could be used for direct comparison. On direct comparison, it can be seen that Brand Positioning (X_3) and Entrepreneurial management (X_4) are more or less equally important variables for Process innovation performance (Y_3). Moreover, relative magnitudes indicate that both Brand Positioning (X_3) and Entrepreneurial management (X_4) have more marked effects than other variables. Thus to the extent that Brand Positioning activities and Entrepreneurial management activities are performed in a much better way than the other variables of SM, represents the most direct way of increasing Process innovation performance (Y_3).

10.6 MODEL 4—Strategic Marketing and System Innovation

Summary of the regression coefficients and significance with respect to model 4, through the confirmatory estimation approach and the stepwise estimation approach are given in Tables 10.8 and 10.9 respectively for both the studies.

Karnataka study
From the confirmatory approach, it can be seen that two variables X_1 and X_4 is statistically significant ($p \leq 0.1$), whereas the stepwise model contains only *one* significant ($p \leq 0.05$) variables i.e. X_4.

The variable X_1 is significant at $p \leq 0.1$, in the confirmatory model and the impact of X_4 is certain. Hence, in the current research we consider Entrepreneurial Management (X_4) as the variable, which has a direct impact on System innovation performance (Y_4). Moreover, the non-significance of all variables other than Environmental Landscaping (X_1) and Entrepreneurial Management (X_4) is leading

Table 10.8 Model 4—Coefficients

Karnataka study						
Model 4	Coefficients	Unstandardized coefficients B	Std. error	Standardized coefficients beta	T	Sig.
(a) Confirmatory estimation approach						
Dependent variable Y_4	Constants	2.232	0.418		5.335	0.000
	X_1	0.182	0.112	0.212	1.616	0.090
	X_2	−0.024	0.110	−0.029	−0.216	0.830
	X_3	0.033	0.078	0.054	0.418	0.677
	X_4	0.316	0.107	0.340	2.963	0.004
(b) Stepwise estimation approach						
Dependent variable Y_4	(Constant)	2.523	0.377		6.692	0.000
	X_4	0.437	0.087	0.470	5.030	0.000

Table 10.9 Model 4—coefficients

Tamil Nadu study						
Model 4	Coefficients	Unstandardized coefficients B	Std. error	Standardized coefficients beta	T	Sig.
(a) Confirmatory estimation approach						
Dependent variable Y_4	Constants	1.998	0.399		4.999	0.000
	X_1	0.177	0.102	0.201	1.897	0.056
	X_2	−0.036	0.123	−0.039	−0.332	0.830
	X_3	0.0056	0.056	0.045	0.336	0.066
	X_4	0.412	0.136	0.441	3.023	0.23
(b) Stepwise estimation approach						
Dependent variable Y_4	(Constant)	2.963	0.412		7.032	0.000
	X_1	0.521	0.065	0.532	4.996	0.000
	X_3	0.665	0.541	0.221	6.551	0.003

to the conclusion that the other variables are not having a direct impact on System innovation performance (Y_4).

In viewing the regression coefficient of the significant variables the sign is an indication of the relationship (positive or negative) between the independent and dependent variables. The significant variables Environmental Landscaping (X_1) and Entrepreneurial Management (X_4) have positive coefficient. This indicates that more positive perceptions of SM, i.e. higher values of Environmental Landscaping (X_1) and Entrepreneurial Management (X_4) increase System innovation performance (Y_4).

The beta coefficients are listed in the column headed standardized coefficients beta, which could be used for direct comparison. On direct comparison, it can be seen that Environmental Landscaping (X_1) and Entrepreneurial management (X_4) are more or less equally important variables for System innovation performance (Y_4). Moreover, relative magnitudes indicate that Entrepreneurial Management (X_4) has a more marked effect, even more than two times, than other variable. Thus to the extent that the organization is highly Entrepreneurial focused than any other variables of SM, represents the most direct way of increasing System innovation performance (Y_4).

Tamil Nadu study

From the confirmatory approach, it can be seen that two variables X_1 and X_3 is statistically significant ($p \leq 0.1$), whereas the stepwise model also contains *two* significant ($p \leq 0.05$) variables i.e. X_1 and X_3.

The variable X_1 is significant at $p \leq 0.1$, in the confirmatory model and the impact of X_3 is certain. Hence, in the current research we consider Brand positioning (X_3) as the variable, which has a direct impact on System innovation performance (Y_4). Moreover, the non-significance of all variables other than Environmental Landscaping (X_1) and Brand positining (X_3) is leading to the conclusion that the other variables are not having a direct impact on System innovation performance (Y_4).

In viewing the regression coefficient of the significant variables the sign is an indication of the relationship (positive or negative) between the independent and dependent variables. The significant variables Environmental Landscaping (X_1) and Brand positioning (X_3) have positive coefficient. This indicates that more positive perceptions of SM, i.e. higher values of Environmental Landscaping (X_1) and Brand positioning (X_3) increase System innovation performance (Y_4).

The beta coefficients are listed in the column headed standardized coefficients beta, which could be used for direct comparison. On direct comparison, it can be seen that Environmental Landscaping (X_1) and Brand positioning (X_3) are more or less equally important variables for System innovation performance (Y_4). Moreover, relative magnitudes indicate that Brand positioning (X_3) has a more marked effect, even more than the other variable. Thus to the extent that the organization is highly brand focused than any other variables of SM, represents the most direct way of increasing System innovation performance (Y_4).

Inference:
Karnataka study:
Environmental landscaping and Entrepreneurial management are significant and by seeing the beta coefficients values, it was found that only the Entrepreneurial management is going to enhance the system innovation.

Tamil Nadu:
Environmental landscaping and Brand positioning are significant and by seeing the beta coefficients values, it was found that only the Brand positioning is going to enhance the system innovation.

10.7 MODEL 5—Strategic Marketing and Innovation Management

Summary of the regression coefficients and significance with respect to model 5, through the confirmatory estimation approach and the stepwise estimation approach are given in Tables 10.10 and 10.11 for both studies respectively.

Table 10.10 Model 5—coefficients

Karnataka study						
Model 5	Coefficients	Unstandardized coefficients B	Std. error	Standardized coefficients beta	T	Sig.
(a) Confirmatory estimation approach						
Dependent variable Y_5	Constants	1.474	0.481		3.063	0.003
	X_1	0.125	0.129	0.122	0.964	0.338
	X_2	0.082	0.126	0.086	0.653	0.516
	X_3	0.045	0.090	0.063	0.504	0.616
	X_4	0.418	0.123	0.379	3.408	0.001
(b) Stepwise estimation approach						
Dependent variable Y_5	(Constant)	1.888	0.435		4.339	0.000
	X_4	0.565	0.100	0.513	5.642	0.000

Table 10.11 Model 5—coefficients

Tamil Nadu study						
Model 5	Coefficients	Unstandardized coefficients B	Std. error	Standardized coefficients beta	T	Sig.
(a) Confirmatory estimation approach						
Dependent variable Y_5	Constants	1.567	0.399		2.996	0.007
	X_1	0.167	0.213	0.145	0.897	0.413
	X_2	0.098	0.198	0.068	0.752	0.05
	X_3	0.053	0.075	0.079	0.499	0.552
	X_4	0.0399	0.201	0.425	3.969	0.02
(b) Stepwise estimation approach						
Dependent variable Y_5	(Constant)	1.587	0.415		5.669	0.000
	X_2	0.456	0.210	0.654	6.012	0.003
	X_4	0.784	0.156	0.499	5.998	0.000

Karnataka study

From the confirmatory approach, it can be seen a variable X_4 is statistically significant ($p \leq 0.05$). The stepwise model also contains the same significant (p 0.05) variable X_4. The same variable is significant in both the approach and the impact of this variable is certain.

Hence, in the current research we consider Entrepreneurial Management is the only variable which has a direct impact on Innovation management performance (Y_5). Moreover, the non-significance of all variables other than Entrepreneurial Management is leading to the conclusion that the other variables are not having a direct impact on Innovation management performance (Y_5).

In viewing the regression coefficient of the significant variables the sign is an indication of the relationship (positive or negative) between the independent and dependent variables. The variable Entrepreneurial Management has positive coefficient and this indicates that more positive perceptions of SM, i.e. higher values of Entrepreneurial Management (X_4) increase Innovation management performance.

The beta coefficients are listed in the column headed standardized coefficients beta, which could be used for direct comparison. On direct comparison, it can be seen that relative magnitudes indicate that Entrepreneurial Management (X_4) has a more marked effect than other variables. Thus to the extent that the organization is highly Entrepreneurial oriented than any other variables of SM, represents the most direct way of increasing Innovation Management performance (Y_5).

Tamil Nadu study

From the confirmatory approach, it can be seen variables X_2 and X_4 is statistically significant ($p \leq 0.05$). The stepwise model also contains the same significant (p 0.05) variables X_2 and X_4. The same variable is significant in both the approach and the impact of this variable is certain.

Hence, in the current research we consider Marketing mix (X_2) and Entrepreneurial management (X_4) are the variables which have a direct impact on Innovation management performance (Y_5). Moreover, the non-significance of all variables other than Marketing mix and Entrepreneurial Management is leading to the conclusion that the other variables are not having a direct impact on Innovation management performance (Y_5).

In viewing the regression coefficient of the significant variables the sign is an indication of the relationship (positive or negative) between the independent and dependent variables. The variables Marketing mix and Entrepreneurial management have positive coefficient and this indicates that more positive perceptions of SM, i.e. higher values of Marketing mix (X_2) and Entrepreneurial management increase Innovation management performance.

The beta coefficients are listed in the column headed standardized coefficients beta, which could be used for direct comparison. On direct comparison, it can be seen that relative magnitudes indicate that Marketing mix (X_2) has a more marked effect than other variables. Thus to the extent that the organization is highly concentrating on marketing mix than any other variables of SM, represents the most direct way of increasing Innovation Management performance (Y_5).

10.8 Overview of Results

The regression results, including the complementary evaluation of the stepwise model assist in addressing the basic research question: What is the impact of Strategic Marketing on Innovation performance? In this context, the following aspects are discussed.

The amount of variance explained by all models range from nearly 50.4–64.1% as given in Chap. 9, which is reproduced here in Table 10.12. From the table we can see that the results support the model validity. These R^2 values are quite substantial enough to motivate Indian organizations for adopting Strategic Marketing as a management model in the future, particularly if they want to achieve a high innovation performance.

In terms of explanation, all the methods arrived at essentially the same results identifying the strong influencers as given in Table 10.13a, b. Increase in any of these independent variables of SM results in the increase in the corresponding dependent variable of innovation performance thus indicating a positive correlation.

Table 10.12 Amount of variance for all models

Models	1	2	3	4	5
R^2 (Karnataka study)	0.571	0.609	0.641	0.504	0.518
R^2 (Tamil Nadu study)	0.529	0.648	0.636	0.506	0.589

Table 10.13 Strong influencers of innovation performance

	Dependent variable		Strongly influencing independent variable		B	Sig.
(a) Karnataka study						
1	Technological innovation	Y_1	Entrepreneurial management	X_4	0.442	0.000
2	Product innovation	Y_2	Marketing mix	X_2	0.233	0.03
			Brand positioning	X_3	0.334	0.002
3	Process innovation	Y_3	Brand positioning	X_3	0.263	0.021
			Entrepreneurial management	X_4	0.304	0.001
4	System innovation	Y_4	Entrepreneurial management	X_4	0.470	0.000
5	Innovation management	Y_5	Entrepreneurial management	X_4	0.513	0.000
(b) Tamil Nadu study						
1	Technological innovation	Y_1	Entrepreneurial management	X_4	0.472	0.000
2	Product innovation	Y_2	Marketing mix	X_2	0.256	0.045
			Brand positioning	X_3	0.302	0.003
			Entrepreneurial management	X_4	0.278	0.084
3	Process innovation	Y_3	Brand positioning	X_3	0.289	0.041
			Entrepreneurial management	X_4	0.335	0.022
4	System innovation	Y_4	Environmental landscaping	X_1	0.532	0.000
			Brand positioning	X_3	0.221	0.003
5	Innovation management	Y_5	Marketing mix	X_2	0.654	0.003
			Entrepreneurial management	X_4	0.513	0.000

Karnataka study

Out of the four variables of Strategic Marketing (SM) considered for measuring its impact on innovation performance as many as three variables viz. Marketing Mix (X_2), Brand Positioning (X_3), and Entrepreneurial Management (X_4) are quite significant and are having a strong impact on the innovation performance of organization. Regarding other variable of SM i.e. Environmental Landscaping(X_1), is not significant even though its coefficient is positive. Sufficient evidence is not there to support its impact on innovation performance.

Tamil Nadu study

Out of the four variables of Strategic Marketing (SM) considered for measuring its impact on innovation performance as many as all the four variables viz. Environemtal Landscaping (X_1), Marketing Mix (X_2), Brand Positioning (X_3), and Entrepreneurial Management (X_4) are quite significant and are having a strong impact on the innovation performance of organization.

Inference:

In case of Karnataka study, only three variables of Strategic marketing i.e. X_2, X_3 and X_4 were having strong impact on the innovation performance of the organizations. Whereas with respect to Tamil Nadu study, all the four variables of SM, i.e. X_1, X_2, X_3 and X_4 were having strong impact on the innovation performance of the organizations.

10.9 General Comparison of All Models

Table 10.14a, b shows the summary of significant coefficients obtained through the stepwise approach for both the studies.

Karnataka study

Across all models, we have seen that the SM variables Marketing Mix (X_2), Brand Positioning (X_3) and Entrepreneurial Management (X_4) are having a positive impact on at least three types of innovation performance. This indicates the substantial contribution of these SM variables in improving the innovation performance of organizations. On the other hand, across all models the SM variables Environmental Landscaping (X_1) is not seen significant. Hence, a strong evidence for the contribution of this SM variable towards the innovation performance of organization could not be traced. Among all the significant SM variables, Marketing Mix (X_2), Brand Positioning (X_3) and Entrepreneurial Management (X_4) has substantial impact on innovation performance, which is indicated by the higher positive coefficient values compared to other variables.

To state that only these Strategic Marketing (SM) variables are creating an impact on Innovation performance would not be a relevant statement considering the more complex patterns of collinearity among variables. These SM variables should be better viewed as representatives of perceptual dimensions, with the other variables in each dimension are considered in any conclusions drawn from the results. Management now has an objective analysis that confirms not only the specific influences of key variables, but also the perceptual dimensions, that must be considered in any form of business planning; regarding strategies aimed at achieving innovation performance through SM. Thus, the results provide management with a framework for developing strategies for improving innovation performance through SM.

Table 10.14 Summary of significant coefficients

	Model 1	Model 2	Model 3	Model 4	Model 5
	Y_1	Y_2	Y_3	Y_4	Y_5
(a) Karnataka study					
X_1	–	–	–	–	–
X_2	–	0.142	–	–	–
X_3	–	0.268	0.298	–	–
X_4	0.591	–	0.370	0.437	0.565
(b) Tamil Nadu study					
X_1	–	0.252	–	0.521	–
X_2	–	0.203	–	–	0.456
X_3	–	0.335	0.245	0.665	–
X_4	0.585	–	0.402	–	0.784

Tamil Nadu study

Across all models, we have seen that the SM variables Brand Positioning (X_3) and Entrepreneurial Management (X_4) are having a positive impact on at least three types of innovation performance. This indicates the substantial contribution of these SM variables in improving the innovation performance of organizations. On the other hand, across all models the SM variables Environmental Landscaping (X_1) and Marketing mix (X_2) are having a positive impact on at least two types of innovation performance. Among all the significant SM variables, Environmental landscaping (X_1), Marketing Mix (X_2), Brand Positioning (X_3) and Entrepreneurial Management (X_4) has substantial impact on innovation performance, which is indicated by the higher positive coefficient values.

To state that only these Strategic Marketing (SM) variables are creating an impact on Innovation performance would not be a relevant statement considering the more complex patterns of collinearity among variables. These SM variables should be better viewed as representatives of perceptual dimensions, with the other variables in each dimension are considered in any conclusions drawn from the results. Management now has an objective analysis that confirms not only the specific influences of key variables, but also the perceptual dimensions, that must be considered in any form of business planning; regarding strategies aimed at achieving innovation performance through SM. Thus, the results provide management with a framework for developing strategies for improving innovation performance through SM.

10.10 Validating the Results

The final task in multiple regression is the validation process of the regression model. The primary concern of this process is to ensure that the results are generalisable to the population and not specific to the sample used in estimation. Secondary concern is the model's transferability to the situations in which it will be used.

Here in our research the split sample validation process is adopted. The split sample method of validation is adopted here wherein, we have divided the sample used for research into two parts (Hair et al. 2007):

1. An estimation sub sample for creating the regression model.
2. The holdout or validation sub sample used to test the equation.

This method is adopted due to reasons; the ability to collect new data is limited by such factors as response rate, cost, time pressures and availability of respondents. Comparison of the split samples has been carried out in the subsequent sections for all the models.

Table 10.15 Model 1 validation

Model 1	Full data	Split 1	Split 2
(a) Karnataka study			
ANOVA significance ($p \leq 0.05$)	0.000	0.000	0.000
R^2	0.571	0.518	0.520
% Variation in R^2		9.3	8.94
Significant coefficients ($p \leq 0.05$)	X_4	X_3, X_4	X_4
Significant coefficients ($p \leq 0.10$)	X_2	X_2	X_2, X_3
(b) Tamil Nadu study			
ANOVA significance ($p \leq 0.05$)	0.000	0.000	0.000
R^2	0.529	0.503	0.511
% Variation in R^2		4.91	3.402
Significant coefficients ($p \leq 0.05$)	X_4	X_2, X_4	X_4
Significant coefficients ($p \leq 0.10$)	X_2, X_4	X_2	X_4

10.10.1 Model 1 Validation

Split sample validation results of model 1 are shown in Table 10.15a, b. In both the split-sample validation analyses, the relationship between the independent variables and the dependent variable was statistically significant ($p \leq 0.05$).

Karnataka study

Comparison of the overall model fit demonstrates a high level of similarity of the results in terms of R^2. The total proportion of variance in the relationship utilizing the full data set was 57.1% compared to 51.8% for the first and 52.0% for the second split sample validation. In both of the split-sample validation analyses, the total proportion of variance in the dependent variable explained by the independent variables was within 9.3% of the variance explained in the model using the full data set (57.1%).

Yet in comparing the individual coefficients some differences do appear. In sample 1, X_3 and X_4 are the significant variables are there but in sample 2; there is a significant variable X_4. The relationship between X_4 and Y_1 was statistically significant for the model using the full data set ($p \leq 0.05$). This relationship in one of the validation analysis also was statistically significant ($p \leq 0.05$). There is a common significant variable X_4 for the full data set as well as for both the split samples at $p \leq 0.05$. This indicates that X_4 has a stronger relationship with Y_1. The split sample validation almost supports the findings of the regression analysis using the full data set.

Tamil Nadu study

Comparison of the overall model fit demonstrates a high level of similarity of the results in terms of R^2. The total proportion of variance in the relationship utilizing the full data set was 52.9% compared to 50.3% for the first and 51.1% for the second split sample validation. In both of the split-sample validation analyses, the total proportion of variance in the dependent variable explained by the independent variables was within 4.91% of the variance explained in the model using the full data set (52.9%).

Yet in comparing the individual coefficients some differences do appear. In sample 1, X_2 and X_4 are the significant variables are there but in sample 2; there is a significant variable X_4. The relationship between X_4 and Y_1 was statistically significant for the model using the full data set ($p \leq 0.05$). This relationship in one of the validation analysis also was statistically significant ($p \leq 0.05$). There is a common significant variable X_4 for the full data set as well as for both the split samples at $p \leq 0.05$. This indicates that X_4 has a stronger relationship with Y_1. The split sample validation almost supports the findings of the regression analysis using the full data set.

10.10.2 Model 2 Validation

Split sample validation results of model 2 are shown in Table 10.16a, b. In both the split-sample validation analyses, the relationship between the independent variables and the dependent variable was statistically significant ($p \leq 0.05$).

Karnataka study

Comparison of the overall model fit demonstrates a high level of similarity of the results in terms of R^2. The total proportion of variance in the relationship utilizing the full data set was 60.9% compared to 62.5% for the first split sample validation and 58.1% for the second split sample validation. In both of the split-sample validation analyses, the total proportion of variance in the dependent variable explained by the independent variables was within 4.6% of the variance explained in the model using the full data set (60.9%).

Table 10.16 Model 2 validation

Model 2	Full data	Split 1	Split 2
(a) Karnataka study			
ANOVA significance ($p \leq 0.05$)	0.000	0.03	0.000
R^2	0.609	0.625	0.581
% Variation in R^2		2.62	4.60
Significant coefficients ($p \leq 0.05$)	X_2, X_3	X_2, X_4	X_3
Significant coefficients ($p \leq 0.10$)	*Nil*	*Nil*	*Nil*
(b) Tamil Nadu study			
ANOVA significance ($p \leq 0.05$)	0.000	0.03	0.000
R^2	0.648	0.636	0.621
% Variation in R^2		1.85	4.166
Significant coefficients ($p \leq 0.05$)	X_2, X_3, X_4	X_2, X_4	X_3, X_4
Significant coefficients ($p \leq 0.10$)	*Nil*	*Nil*	*Nil*

Yet in comparing the individual coefficients some differences do appear. In sample 1, there exists two significant variables X_2 and X_4, but in sample 2 there is a significant variable X_3, which is significant at $p \leq 0.05$. There is a common significant variable X_2 and X_3 and for the full data set as well as both the split samples at $p \leq 0.05$. This indicates that X_2 and X_3 has a stronger relationship with Y_2. The split sample validation almost supports the findings of the regression analysis using the full data set.

Tamil Nadu study

Comparison of the overall model fit demonstrates a high level of similarity of the results in terms of R^2. The total proportion of variance in the relationship utilizing the full data set was 64.8% compared to 63.6% for the first split sample validation and 62.1% for the second split sample validation. In both of the split-sample validation analyses, the total proportion of variance in the dependent variable explained by the independent variables was within 4.16% of the variance explained in the model using the full data set (64.8%).

Yet in comparing the individual coefficients some differences do appear. In sample 1, there exists two significant variables X_2 and X_4, but in sample 2, significant variable X_3 and X_4 are significant at $p \leq 0.05$. There is a common significant variable X_2, X_3 and X_4 and for the full data set as well as both the split samples at $p \leq 0.05$. This indicates that X_2, X_3 and X_4 has a stronger relationship with Y_2. The split sample validation almost supports the findings of the regression analysis using the full data set.

10.10.3 Model 3 Validation

Split sample validation results of model 3 are shown in Table 10.17a, b. In both the split-sample validation analyses, the relationship between the independent variables and the dependent variable was statistically significant ($p \leq 0.05$).

Karnataka study

Comparison of the overall model fit demonstrates a high level of similarity of the results in terms of R^2. The total proportion of variance in the relationship utilizing the full data set was 64.1% compared to 62.2% in the first split sample validation and it is 63.0% in the second split sample validation. In both of the split-sample validation analyses, the total proportion of variance in the dependent variable explained by the independent variables was within 2.97% of the variance explained in the model using the full data set (64.1%).

Yet in comparing the individual coefficients some differences do appear. In sample 1, a significant variable X_4 exists and in sample 2, there are significant variables X_3 and X_4, which is significant at $p \leq 0.05$. This indicates that X_3 and X_4

Table 10.17 Model 3 validation

Model 3	Full data	Split 1	Split 2
(a) Karnataka study			
ANOVA significance ($p \leq 0.05$)	0.000	0.000	0.000
R^2	0.641	0.622	0.630
% Variation in R^2		2.97	1.80
Significant coefficients ($p \leq 0.05$)	X_3, X_4	X_4	X_3, X_4
Significant coefficients ($p \leq 0.10$)	*Nil*	X_1	X_2
(b) Tamil Nadu study			
ANOVA significance ($p \leq 0.05$)	0.000	0.000	0.000
R^2	0.636	0.610	0.619
% Variation in R^2		4.08	2.67
Significant coefficients ($p \leq 0.05$)	X_3, X_4	X_4	X_3, X_4
Significant coefficients ($p \leq 0.10$)	*Nil*	X_1	X_2

has a stronger relationship with Y_3. The split sample validation almost supports the findings of the regression analysis using the full data set.

Tamil Nadu study
Comparison of the overall model fit demonstrates a high level of similarity of the results in terms of R^2. The total proportion of variance in the relationship utilizing the full data set was 63.6% compared to 61.0% in the first split sample validation and it is 61.9% in the second split sample validation. In both of the split-sample validation analyses, the total proportion of variance in the dependent variable explained by the independent variables was within 4.08% of the variance explained in the model using the full data set (63.6%).

Yet in comparing the individual coefficients some differences do appear. In sample 1, a significant variable X_4 exists and in sample 2, there are significant variables X_3 and X_4, which is significant at $p \leq 0.05$. This indicates that X_3 and X_4 has a stronger relationship with Y_3. The split sample validation almost supports the findings of the regression analysis using the full data set.

10.10.4 Model 4 Validation

Split sample validation results of model 4 are shown in Table 10.18a, b. In both the split-sample validation analyses, the relationship between the independent variables and the dependent variable was statistically significant ($p \leq 0.05$).

Karnataka study
Comparison of the overall model fit demonstrates a high level of similarity of the results in terms of R^2. The total proportion of variance in the relationship utilizing the full data set was 50.4% compared to 52.1% for the first split sample validation and 48.5% for the second split sample validation. In both of the split-sample validation analyses, the total proportion of variance in the dependent variable

Table 10.18 Model 4 validation

Model 4	Full data	Split 1	Split 2
(a) Karnataka study			
ANOVA significance ($p \leq 0.05$)	0.000	0.000	0.000
R^2	0.504	0.521	0.485
% Variation in R^2		3.37	3.8
Significant coefficients ($p \leq 0.05$)	X_4	X_1, X_4	X_4
Significant coefficients ($p \leq 0.10$)	X_1	*Nil*	X_8
(b) Tamil Nadu study			
ANOVA significance ($p \leq 0.05$)	0.000	0.000	0.000
R^2	0.506	0.519	0.498
% Variation in R^2		2.56	1.59
Significant coefficients ($p \leq 0.05$)	X_1, X_3	X_1, X_3	X_3
Significant coefficients ($p \leq 0.10$)	X_1	*Nil*	X_3

explained by the independent variables was within 3.8% of the variance explained in the model using the full data set (50.4%).

Comparing the individual coefficients also reveals similarity. In sample 1, sample 2, and the full data set, X_5 has emerged as a strong significant variable ($p \leq 0.05$). This indicates that X_4 has a very strong relationship with Y_4. The split sample validation almost supports the findings of the regression analysis using the full data set.

Tamil Nadu study

Comparison of the overall model fit demonstrates a high level of similarity of the results in terms of R^2. The total proportion of variance in the relationship utilizing the full data set was 50.6% compared to 51.9% for the first split sample validation and 49.8% for the second split sample validation. In both of the split-sample validation analyses, the total proportion of variance in the dependent variable explained by the independent variables was within 2.56% of the variance explained in the model using the full data set (50.6%).

Comparing the individual coefficients also reveals similarity. In sample 1, sample 2, and the full data set, X_1 and X_3 has emerged as a strong significant variables ($p \leq 0.05$). This indicates that X_1 and X_3 has a very strong relationship with Y_4. The split sample validation almost supports the findings of the regression analysis using the full data set.

10.10.5 Model 5 Validation

Split sample validation results of model 5 are shown in Table 10.19a, b. In both the split-sample validation analyses, the relationship between the independent variables and the dependent variable was statistically significant ($p \leq 0.05$).

Table 10.19 Model 5 validation

Model 5	Full data	Split 1	Split 2
(a) Karnataka study			
ANOVA significance ($p \leq 0.05$)	0.000	0.000	0.000
R^2	0.518	0.532	0.488
% Variation in R^2		2.70	5.88
Significant coefficients ($p \leq 0.05$)	X_4	X_4	X_3, X_4
Significant coefficients ($p \leq 0.10$)	*Nil*	*Nil*	*Nil*
(b) Tamil Nadu study			
ANOVA significance ($p \leq 0.05$)	0.000	0.000	0.000
R^2	0.589	0.597	0.567
% Variation in R^2		1.35	3.73
Significant coefficients ($p \leq 0.05$)	X_2 X_4	X_4	X_2, X_4
Significant coefficients ($p \leq 0.10$)	*Nil*	*Nil*	*Nil*

Karnataka study
Comparison of the overall model fit demonstrates a high level of similarity of the results in terms of R^2. The total proportion of variance in the relationship utilizing the full data set was 51.8% compared to 53.2% for the first split sample validation and 48.8% for the second split sample validation. In both of the split-sample validation analyses, the total proportion of variance in the dependent variable explained by the independent variables was within 5.88% of the variance explained in the model using the full data set (51.8%).

Yet in comparing the individual coefficients some differences do appear. In sample 1 X_4 is a significant variable and in sample 2 there are two significant variables X_3 and X_4, which is significant at $p \leq 0.05$. There is a common significant variable X_4 for the full data set as well as both the split samples at $p \leq 0.05$. This indicates that X_4 has a stronger relationship with Y_2. The split sample validation almost supports the findings of the regression analysis using the full data set.

Tamil Nadu study
Comparison of the overall model fit demonstrates a high level of similarity of the results in terms of R^2. The total proportion of variance in the relationship utilizing the full data set was 58.9% compared to 59.7% for the first split sample validation and 56.7% for the second split sample validation. In both of the split-sample validation analyses, the total proportion of variance in the dependent variable explained by the independent variables was within 3.73% of the variance explained in the model using the full data set (58.9%).

Yet in comparing the individual coefficients some differences do appear. In sample 1 X_4 is a significant variable and in sample 2 there are two significant variables X_2 and X_4, which is significant at $p \leq 0.05$. There significant variables X_2

and X_4 for the full data set as well as both the split samples at $p \leq 0.05$. This indicates that X_2 and X_4 has a stronger relationship with Y_2. The split sample validation almost supports the findings of the regression analysis using the full data set.

10.11 Summary

The summary of validation for all models is given in Table 10.20a, b. All the models are statistically significant indicated by the ANOVA significance values. The percentage variation in R^2 is within 5% for 3 models and within 10% for 2 models. Though minor differences in the significant variables are seen, split samples has either yielded the significant variables of the full data set or not yielded any significant variable. None of the split samples models has added a new significant variable different from the full data set. From the summary it can be seen that by and large all the five models exhibit validity and could be generalized.

In this chapter, all the final regression models developed were interpreted and discussed based on the regression coefficients and their significance. The models were also subjected to a validation analysis and the validation results were discussed. These discussions gave a detailed insight into the research objectives under investigation done for both Karnataka and Tamil Nadu studies.

Table 10.20 Summary of validation

Model	1	2	3	4	5
(a) Karnataka study					
Significance ($p \leq 0.05$) maximum	0.000	0.03	0.000	0.000	0.000
% Variation in R^2 *(split 1)*	9.30	2.62	2.97	3.37	2.70
% Variation in R^2 *(split 2)*	8.94	4.60	1.80	3.80	5.88
Common significant coefficients ($p \leq 0.05$)	X_4	X_2, X_3	X_3, X_4	X_4	X_4
Common significant coefficients ($p \leq 0.1$)	X_2	*Nil*	*Nil*	*Nil*	*Nil*
(b) Tamil Nadu study					
Significance ($p \leq 0.05$) maximum	0.000	0.03	0.041	0.003	0.003
% Variation in R^2 *(split 1)*	4.91	1.85	4.08	2.56	1.35
% Variation in R^2 *(split 2)*	3.402	4.166	2.62	1.59	3.73
Common significant coefficients ($p \leq 0.05$)	X_2, X_4	X_2, X_3, X_4	X_3, X_4	X_3	X_4
Common significant coefficients ($p \leq 0.1$)	X_4	*Nil*	*Nil*	*Nil*	*Nil*

10.12 Conclusions

Focusing on the Objectives of the Research

Strategic Marketing as a strategy to improve competitiveness has been adopted, for long by Indian organizations, which was the need of the liberalized and globalized scenario. In the fast changing technological era, with growing competition in the market place, customers have become more demanding and to remain competitive, organizations constantly need to improve their innovation performance in all their activities, in addition to ensuring their product and service quality. It was in this context that this research was taken up with the primary intention of investigating the impact of Strategic Marketing on the innovation performance of organizations. We have attempted to explore this through a systematic research process. The research had specific objectives as outlined and the research objectives have been achieved as described below:

Building the measures of Strategic Marketing and Innovation and develop a conceptual research framework for examining the relationship between them.

In Chap. 5, through a systematic approach to research design, we developed the measures of Strategic Marketing (SM) and innovation performance. Four constructs of SM and five constructs of innovation performance were developed for measurement. A conceptual research framework which depicts the scope of the research; the relationships, which are planned to be explored, and the various dimensions of SM and innovation performance which are subjected to investigation was developed.

Designing a measuring instrument using Strategic Marketing and Innovation measures and check for its reliability and validity (testing the instrument).

In Chap. 6 through a systematic approach of concept development, specification of concept dimensions and selection of indicators, a questionnaire to collect primary data from organizations was done as a pilot study. The reliability and the validity of the measuring instrument were established here. Further, in Chap. 7, it was discussed in detail on the data reduction and confirmatory factor analysis done for the main study. Chapter 8 gives more details about the preliminary data analysis methodology used for the collected primary data and the hypotheses testing. Further, in Chap. 7, a confirmatory factor analysis was also carried out on the collected data to strengthen the validity of the measuring instrument. A summated scale was created by combining variables highly loading on factors and averaging it.

Examine the relationship between Strategic Marketing and Innovation and also its impact on each.

After doing a preliminary data analysis in Chap. 8, detailed discussions on establishing the relationship between the variables under study i.e. SM and innovation performance by the method of multiple regression analysis was carried out in Chap. 9. The hypothesis testing of the five models developed here was carried out for verifying the relationship between the variables under study. The impact of SM on innovation performance of organizations was statistically established, by a series of systematic data analysis using multiple regression, ensuring the compliance to the assumption requirements for the analysis.

Examine the effect of different dimensions of Innovation on Strategic marketing dimensions and find which of these needs more thrust in an organization.

To make appropriate suggestions on the need for adoption of SM as a means for any Indian manufacturing organizations to achieve a higher growth rate.

This chapter discusses each of the five models developed individually to investigate the impact of different dimensions of SM on different types of innovation performance and identifies the relevant and important variables of SM, which needs more emphasis within the organization. It was suggested that the organizations are to concentrate on the significant and important variables of SM, which influences the innovation performance within the organizations. To strengthen the findings, further a split sample validation of the various models was also carried out which enabled to generalize the results.

Important Findings From Both Karnataka and Tamil Nadu Studies

A detailed insight into the various variables involved in Strategic marketing (SM) and innovation performance within an organization were obtained through this research. These variables describe an organization's strategic marketing and Innovation performances to a large extent, which is backed by exhaustive literature and investigations.

A reliable and valid questionnaire (measuring instrument) to assess the SM and innovation performance was developed. Hence, the results of statistical data analysis of the data collected using this questionnaire becomes trustworthy.

The relationship established between SM and innovation performance clearly indicates that SM in general has a strong impact on the innovation performance of an organization, irrespective of the type of innovation. Hence, achieving SM performance can lead to achieve innovation performance also within an organization.

The research exhibits the important role played by the Entrepreneurial Management, which is an element of SM for the improved Technological innovation performance as well as the Process Innovation, System Innovation and Innovation management performance within an organization. This conclusion with respect to Karnataka study emphasizes the need to strengthen the Entrepreneurial management activities like development of new products or new Business ideas, its deployment and its monitoring. In addition to this, the result from Tamil Nadu study indicates that entrepreneurial management also improves the product innovation of an organization.

Marketing mix and Brand positioning being an important element of SM, has a significant role in improving the product and process innovation performance of the organization and needs to be strengthened. In addition to these activities, Entrepreneurial management is directed towards improving Process innovation within an organization. The research revealed that the effect of Marketing mix, Brand positioning and Entrepreneurial management activities could improve the product or process innovation with respect to Karnataka study. The same inference is obtained with respect to Tamil Nadu counterpart.

The impact of Entrepreneurial management, which is an element of SM on system innovation and innovation management, is significant. Growth oriented organizations lay a lot of emphasis on entrepreneurial management.

In a general comparison, it can be seen that, out of the four variables of SM considered, as many as three variables like Marketing Mix, Brand Positioning and Entrepreneurial Management are having a significant impact in one way or the other way on the overall innovation performance of the organization with respect to Karnataka study. The same result is observed from Tamil Nadu study.

Across all relationship models in both Karnataka and Tamil Nadu studies, significant evidence for the contribution of the SM variable Environmental landscaping towards innovation performance is very little. Relatively Tamil Nadu study demonstrates a little impact of environmental landscaping as with respect to that of Karnataka study. This does not necessarily mean that this variable is not at all contributing to the innovation performance but contribute with a very weak significance.

The substantial impact of Marketing mix, Brand positioning and Entrepreneurial management is a strong evidence to support the argument, that innovation is basically Market, Brand and Entrepreneurial dependent wherein Strategic Marketing also emphasizes these aspects. Some of the common ideas of SM and innovation well revealed by the research consist of, the need for considering Marketing mix, Brand positioning and Entrepreneurial oriented activities to be taken for achieving competitive advantage. This inference is applicable both for Karnataka and Tamil Nadu studies.

10.13 Limitations of the Research

Of course, our research is not free from its limitations. The limitations of the research are identified as given below:

1. A substantial review of literature has been carried out and the research relies very much on these available resources through IISc and internet. Though utmost care was taken to include all the relevant variables involved, it may not be exhaustive.
2. This ex post facto research is an empirical study, involving primary data collection from organization and its statistical analysis by multivariate techniques. Attempts were made to investigate the perceptions of organizations on their experience with practicing of Strategic Marketing (SM) and innovation performance.
3. The research is not an experimental research involving the investigation of the concepts of SM and innovation from their first principles. Hence, all the limitations applicable to multivariate statistical techniques are applicable here.

4. Sampling for the statistical analysis is taken from a selected group of Micro, Small and medium scale manufacturing organizations of Indian origin in Karnataka and Tamil Nadu. Utmost care has been exercised while sampling, to ensure a fair representativeness even though the sampling methodology is non-probability sampling based on judgmental and purposive sampling.
5. Getting the feedback on the questionnaire has been a real task as far as primary data collection is concerned. The process of evaluation adopted by means of the questionnaire was a type of self-assessment exercise wherein the respondents are assessing their own organization.
6. Even though the collected primary data may be sufficient for purposes of analysis, getting more data and responses from organizations is limited by various factors ranging from reluctance to disclose information, respondent's inability to devote time, lack of enthusiasm etc. to simple non-response. Response rate has limited the sample size leading to difficulties in accurate generalizations. More over invalid data and data that do not meet the assumption requirements of statistical analysis had to be eliminated for the purpose of data analysis and getting the model fit.

10.14 Direction for Future Research

1. The direction for the future research originates from the results of this research and its limitations. Future research should explore the existence of any other variables, which are not covered in this research.
2. The research has given the findings in terms of, which dimensions of Strategic Marketing (SM) are influencing which type of innovation. To understand more, a detailed study on each one of these relationships and the reasons underlying them can be taken up separately by a case study approach.
3. This research excludes organizations belonging to the category of service enterprises. In addition, organizations who have not adopted any SM practice who do not fall under the sampling frame are excluded. This research study could be replicated and refined in other research contexts covering this category.
4. Due to practical limitations, the sampling plan for the research was not a random sampling even though utmost care was taken to ensure due representation. Future research may be taken up by exploring the possibility of random sampling.
5. Since the questionnaire used was a self-evaluation tool, a direction for future research can be a comparison of this evaluation with the stakeholder evaluation.
6. The Multiple regression is used to analyze the data in our present work, SEM (Structural Equation Modeling) may be used further to do the data analysis.

10.15 End Notes

It is important to recognize that a single study is not a final word in true spirit. This study is through successive stages of model formulation, systematic data analysis, and refinement has given certain conclusions on the impact of Strategic Marketing (SM) on the innovation performance of organizations. Such an analysis can be considered as a preliminary finding in exploring the impact of SM on innovation performance within organizations. The confidence and assurance in such a research design and measurement scheme cannot be obtained through analytical rigor alone. In that matter, the present research findings could be used as guidelines for further research.

For many business organizations especially manufacturing organizations, the competitive scenario has changed significantly in the past few years. Due to rapid changes happening both at the local and global level, customer's requirements are becoming very dynamic with respect to its quality, technology and innovative features to make a product success. All these things can be achieved through several strategies that a firm can suitably adopt to gain the competitive advantage. This research can be a boon and definitely of greater help in formulating the future strategies for the Indian manufacturing organizations.

10.16 Review Questions

1. How do you interpret the regression variate and coefficient for the current research work?
2. Explain how you build the predictive equation for models based on the confirmatory approach in this study.
3. Elaborate on the validation of the results obtained in the current study and also highlight the important findings of the work.
4. Elaborate on the limitations and future research directions for the current study.

Reference

Hair JF Jr, Black WC, Babin BJ, Anderson RE, Tatham RL (2007) Multivariate data analysis, 6th edn. Pearson Prentice Hall (Chaps. 1, 2 & 4)

Annexure-I

Questionnaire

Strategic Marketing and Innovation Performance of Organisations: A Study on Indian MSMEs

Dear Sir,

We understand that your organization has been implementing Strategic Marketing practices and are successful in business. We are interested in finding out the impact of this Strategic Marketing practices on the Innovation performance of your organization. In this connection we hereby request your kind cooperation in collecting data related to Strategic Marketing and Innovation from your organization. We hereby assure that the collected data will be purely used for academic purposes only and due confidentiality will be maintained.

The data is required in the form of a feedback to a questionnaire attached herewith. Responding to the questionnaire is extremely simple where in you are requested to give the level of agreement with respect to a statement made with respect to your esteemed organization in a scale of 1–5.

If you **STRONGLY AGREE** to statement give a score of **5**

If you **SOME WHAT AGREE** to a statement give a score of **4**

If you have a **NEUTRAL OPINION**, neither agree nor disagree then give **3**

If you **SOME WHAT DISAGREE** with the statement then give a score of **2**

If you **STRONGLY DISAGREE** with the statement then give a score of **1**

R. Srinivasan and C.P. Lohith, *Strategic Marketing and Innovation for Indian MSMEs*, India Studies in Business and Economics,
DOI 10.1007/978-981-10-3590-6

PART 1
Basic Information

Name of Organization:
Products/Services of Organization:
Address:
Name of Senior Manager(s):
Designation(s):
Type of manufacturing organization (tick): General engineering/Textiles and Garments/Electrical and Electronics/Printing and Stationery/Rubber and Plastics/Chemicals/Food and Beverages/Basic metal/Any other
Size of Organization (tick): Micro Scale/Small Scale/Medium Scale
Strategic marketing initiatives of organization (tick): Definition of companies product markets/vision and mission statement/New Product development/Branding/Long-term investment/Forecast of Technological changes/Merger and Acquisitions/Any other

MSME Classification:

Sector	Micro enterprises	Small enterprises	Medium enterprises
Manufacturing	Up to Rs. 25 Lakhs	Above Rs. 25 Lakhs but does not exceed Rs. 5 Crores	Above Rs. 5 Crores but does not exceed Rs. 10 Crores

PART 2
Statements Describing Strategic Marketing

1. Environmental Landscaping (X_1)	
1	We have developed strategies to maintain and build a good customer relationship
2	We have effective means to determine customer expectations
3	We have developed effective means (surveys, visits) to measure the level of customer satisfaction with all processes that affect customer expectations
4	We prefer to have a good relationship with our competitors
5	We consider competitors as the source of inspirations for our growth
6	We initiate strategic orientations among suppliers
7	We take all legal aspects into considerations thorough out our business
8	We ensure that our organization follow the environment protection laws to the great extent
9	We focus on protecting the Technology through patent protection
10	Our firm insists us to commercialise the product from lab to the market place
11	We take all measures to improve the productivity of our organization
12	We gave at most importance for the employee career growth

2. Marketing Mix—4Ps (X_2)	
1	Our goal is to manufacture a superior quality product
2	We give innovative features in order to remain competitive in the market
3	Our customer will have wide number of product options (variants)
4	We give more importance for the external appearance of our products
5	Our goal is to provide a good service to the products we manufacture
6	We ensure a high warranty for our products
7	We use all the channels to see our products reach wide locations
8	We follow a good and effective logistics in meeting the customer demands
9	We adopt innovative ways of advertising our products
10	We give more importance for wide publicity of our products
11	We follow various sales promotional strategies to sell our products
12	We often consider pricing strategy as one of the way to increase sales of our products
3. Brand Positioning—(X_3)	
1	We agree that Brand positioning strengthens product image to a great extent
2	Our primary focus is to build brand equity (set of assets or liabilities associated with a brand)
3	We consider that the products that perform beyond customer expectations increase brand image
4	We adopt consistent advertising strategy to enhance brand positioning
5	We believe in distribution effectiveness i.e. customer exposed to the brand when shopping helps in Brand positioning
6	We adopt an effective brand (trade mark) since it evokes feeling of security, trust and confidence among customers
7	We consider perceived quality as a mode of positioning brand effectively since it reduces cost of retaining customers
8	We consider Brand awareness as one of the important element which helps in the Brand positioning
9	We believe that Branding increases customer loyalty
10	We consider that Branding plays an important role in building relationships with customers
11	We believe that Branding helps firms in getting higher returns
12	We believe that Branding must attract and keep customer by promoting value, image, prestige and lifestyle
4. Entrepreneurial Management (X_4)	
1	We believe that various attributes of entrepreneurship like education and prior experience enhances the capability of identifying opportunities in the market
2	We strongly focus on coordinating marketing with manufacturing, distribution, operations, financial and other decisions
3	We strongly adopt entrepreneurial skills to launch and develop a New product
4	We believe strategic planning and marketing is needed for the growth of an enterprise
5	We explore new avenues among the available resources for the growth of our business

(continued)

(continued)

4. Entrepreneurial Management (X_4)	
6	We take risks while exploiting the available resources to develop innovative products
7	We motivate our employees to utilise their talent and available resources effectively for the improved productivity of our organisation
8	We often encourage our employees to exhibit their entrepreneurial skills in accomplishing short term and long term goals of an organisation
9	We consider entrepreneurial management as an effective action taken for the specific needs of MSME's
10	We often consider entrepreneurial management as a way to identify and exploit opportunities for acquiring and retaining profitable customers
11	We strongly believe that through entrepreneurial orientation, firm achieves to acquire competitive advantage
12	We believe that increase in the entrepreneurial activities by the firms helps its economic growth

PART 3
Statements Describing Innovation Practices and Performance

1. Technological Innovation (Y_1)	
1	Our organization always attempts to stay on the leading edge of new technology in our industry
2	We make an effort to anticipate the full potential of new practices and technologies
3	We pursue long-range programmes in order to acquire technological capabilities in advance of our needs
4	We are constantly thinking of the next generation of technology
5	Our processes are improved using innovation and creativity
6	We have excellent communication processes between R&D and other departments
7	Our R&D pursues truly innovative and leading-edge research
8	Our R&D strategy is mainly characterized by high risk projects with chance of high return
9	In our organization R&D plays a major part in our building our business strategy
10	We believe that Technological innovations are helping our organization to develop new products
2. Product Innovation (Y_2)	
1	The levels of newness (novelty) of our new products are really new to the Industry
2	We use the latest technologies in new product development
3	Our response to technology and customer are faster and the speed of new product development is much faster
4	In our industry we are ahead in the number of new products introduced to the market
5	Out of all the new products introduced we have the maximum number of new products that is first-to-market (early market entrants)
6	We emphasize Quality over cost in product design

(continued)

(continued)

2. Product Innovation (Y_2)	
7	We design products to customers' requirements
8	Whatever new product or new service introduced by us entirely new to industry
9	We always experiment with use of new materials or intermediate products
10	We identify a new functional solution for an existing product or additional service based on an existing service
3. Process Innovation (Y_3)	
1	The processes used by us are updated and novel
2	We are much faster in the adoption of the latest technologies in processes
3	In our organization the rate of change in processes, techniques and technology are much faster
4	We adopt the newest method of production/service delivery
5	We have commercialized creative ideas into processes/products/services
6	We frequently introduce new products and services
7	We frequently develop new operational processes
8	We frequently adopt experimentation and flexible routines for the improved process innovation
9	We believe that the innovation will be positively impacted by process improvement
10	We strongly believe that more competitive environment needs the frequent changes in process
4. System Innovation (Y_4)	
1	We strive to be a learning organization
2	We create long-term goals
3	We manage innovation proactively
4	We make innovation a part of our strategy
5	We create opportunities for cross-functional collaboration
6	Our organization encourages and teach teamwork
7	We encourage the use of problem-solving skills
8	We teach people to assess their creative potential
9	We always take steps to overcome barriers to creativity
10	We identify market opportunities and enter a new market
5. Innovation Management (Y_5)	
1	Our top management always supports new ideas
2	Our organization develops the creative capability of individuals
3	Our organization has built a creative culture by encouragement and support
4	Our organization access new ideas from external sources
5	In our organization the staff is updated with best practice Learning
6	We have an organizational structure to support creativity
7	Our management is committed for innovation

(continued)

(continued)

5. Innovation Management (Y_5)	
8	Our organization has allocated specific budgets for innovative ideas
9	In our organization evaluation of technical, economic and commercial feasibility of innovative ideas are carried out
10	In our organization information system acts as a stimulus for new ideas

Thank You

Index

R. Srinivasan and C.P. Lohith, *Strategic Marketing and Innovation for Indian MSMEs*, India Studies in Business and Economics,
DOI 10.1007/978-981-10-3590-6

The manufacturer's authorised representative in the EU is Springer Nature Customer Service Centre GmbH, Europaplatz 3, 69115 Heidelberg, Germany. If you have any concerns regarding our products, please contact ProductSafety@springernature.com

Printed and bound by CPI Group (UK) Ltd, Croydon, CR0 4YY
30/09/2026
02225470-0009